Samira and Samir

The Author

Born in Iran, Siba Shakib grew up in Tehran and attended a German school there. A writer and maker of documentaries and films, she has travelled to Afghanistan many times in recent years, visiting the north as well as the territory commanded by the Taliban. Several of her documentaries have won awards, including the moving testimonials she has made of the horrors of life in Afghanistan and the plight of the Afghan women. She is currently working on translating her books into films, and advising ISAS, the peacekeeping force in Afghanistan. When not travelling the world with her work, she lives in New York and Germany.

Also by Siba Shakib

Afghanistan, Where God Only Comes to Weep

Samira and Samir

Siba Shakib

Century · London

Published by Century in 2004

1 3 5 7 9 10 8 6 4 2

First published in the United Kingdom in 2004 by Century
The Random House Group Limited
20 Vauxhall Bridge Road, London SW1V 2SA

Random House Australia (Pty) Limited
20 Alfred Street, Milsons Point, Sydney,
New South Wales 2061, Australia

Random House New Zealand Limited
18 Poland Road, Glenfield,
Auckland 10, New Zealand

Random House South Africa (Pty) Limited
Endulini, 5a Jubilee Road, Parktown 2193, South Africa

The Random House Group Limited Reg. No. 954009

www.randomhouse.co.uk

A CIP catalogue record for this book is available
from the British Library

Papers used by Random House are natural,
recyclable products made from wood grown in sustainable forests.
The manufacturing processes conform to the environmental
regulations of the country of origin

ISBN 1 8441 3453 9

Typeset in Fairfield by SX Composing DTP, Rayleigh, Essex
Printed and bound in the Great Britain by
Clays Ltd, St. Ives Plc, Bungay, Suffolk

For my father,
my brothers,
and their sons.
For those who fell
and those who did not.

If you have a secret, take it,
carry it to the Hindu Kush
and lay it beneath a stone

A GIRL

Is he dead?

Don't worry. He is as much alive as you and I.

Are you sure?

God in heaven, why should he be dead?

If he is not dead, why is he not saying anything?

Daria wants to reply, cannot, clenches her teeth, bends double.

The commander does not see his lovely wife's pain, he wants an answer from her.

Daria does not want the people in the other tents to hear her. She chokes back the cry in her throat. The taste of blood comes into her mouth, frightens her. She loses the colour from her face.

Answer me, says the commander.

Leave me in peace. Daria hisses her words like a snake. She has hardly spoken them, when she already regrets it. Although he is squatting on the ground behind her, Daria sees it. The commander is startled like a child, shudders, tenses up, wraps his arms around his knees, lowers his eyes, makes himself small, goes quiet.

Daria does not like it when she loses her temper and scolds her husband. She turns around to him, smiles despite her pain, says, be patient. God is great. He will provide. She speaks quietly. Because it is important what she has to say. Because no one else should hear it. Only her commander.

He raises his eyes, lowers them again. Swallows. He no longer hugs his knees, but with his finger paints pictures on the mud floor. Invisible pictures. My son is to be called Samir, he says, and smiles. A smile half sad, half grateful, which only Daria knows. Before her the commander's dead mother knew this smile. It is not a man's smile. It is the smile of a little boy. The commander has brought it from his childhood, from a time that he knows as Before, into his life as a man.

Before is long gone. The commander is a warrior, a protector, someone invincible, people say, lowering their voices, looking around. And if the commander is not nearby they say, but there is one pain he can not bear, that is the pain that comes when his wife is angry with him and scolds him.

No one knows that better than Daria herself. It would kill her commander if she stopped giving him the love he needs. Daria is afraid of that. Of his death and her guilt. So she gives him everything he needs so that he can be strong, so that he can be an honest and a God-fearing man, a knowledgable and a just commander. So that he can be a kind father to their children. Daria gives him what he needs so that she does not lose his protection.

Samir is a pretty name, says Daria, then bends double and straightens again. Her back becomes a desert, her muscles hills of sand, which allow the wind to carry them here and there. The commander hears all of Daria's words. The spoken and the unspoken.

Daria squats on the floor, sees nothing, only the fire in the oven-hole and the pot on top of it in which the water is boiling. It speaks to her, as it simmers and scolds. Daria replies. The bubbles are cheeky and brave, jump out of the pot. Some of them Daria catches in the air. Some of them jump into the fire. Stupid bubbles, Daria says half to herself, half to the water in the pot. Stupid bubbles that jump into the fire just to die there. With a hiss. Stupid like the men, like the warriors, stupid like my own husband, the commander, who goes to war just to kill and, the day will come, to be killed himself.

At first the commander thought Daria was betraying him. After days away at war he returned to his high plain, heard voices in his tent. He thought his wife had been letting people into his tent behind his back. He jumped from his horse, sneaked up, drew his dagger, entered the tent and was surprised to find his wife alone. I didn't know you spoke the language of water, he said, and squatted next to his Daria, looking in turn at the water and his wife.

However much he listens and tries, until today the commander can not understand the words that his Daria babbles. At first he wanted to bring her back to her father, because he thought she had lost her mind. After all, no one with all their senses talks to water. Then he thought, it is better that she talks to the water than to strange men.

Carefully, very carefully, just as he did before, when he was a little boy and first stretched his hand out towards the hot flames in the fire, as though his hand is a snake creeping along, the commander stretches out his fingers.

He wants to touch his Daria's back, but she raises her voice again, talks to the water and the bubbles. Like a startled snake, the commander draws back his hand. Daria wails and groans, clenches her teeth so that the commander hears them crunch and crack. Daria bends double, holds her fat belly, reaches between her legs, she feels her son's head, her fingers slip.

The commander reaches to the side, finds the fresh, warm bread, pulls a piece off, puts it in his mouth and chews on it. Not because he is hungry, more to chase the fear from his head. Before she crouched down to pull his son out of her body, his hard-working water-wife pulled the bread out of the oven-hole in the tent floor. So that it will not burn, flour is expensive, she said, then crouched down and said, my son does not want to be in my belly any more, he wants out of my body.

Daria scratches open the floor beneath her, pushes the earth aside and digs a little trough so that she has enough room underneath her.

You are like my mother, says the commander, goes on chewing on his bread.

I am like the commander's mother, says Daria.

Not a day passes without you pulling something or other out of somewhere, says the commander. Women are always pulling all sorts of things out of somewhere. Today, you first pulled the fishes out of the water, then the thorn out of my hand, then the bread out of the oven, and now you are about to pull my son out of your body. The commander sees his wife's back and says something he has never said to her before. The only thing you will never be able to pull out is the longing for you that I carry inside me.

Daria wipes the sweat from her brow, says, my mother

said men respect their wives only for as long as they pull sons out of their bodies for them.

That is true, says the commander, but it is also true that I wanted you even before I rode to you and got you from your father's house. Even before anyone had told me about you, before I buried my face in your black hair, before I knew your fragrance. The commander runs his finger over the bumps of her back and says, my longing for you began to live and grow within me the first time I heard your name. Daria, the sea, the river.

That had been the day when his father put him in charge of twelve of his men. From today you are a commander, his father said, embraced his son and sent him into battle. All day the young commander and his men had chased the enemy. At one point one side was firing their guns, at another point the other. At one point one had the upper hand, then the other. They were scared, they were having doubts, they were losing their courage, they were killing. By the time the sun disappeared behind the mountain, the young commander had defeated the enemy. He returned with his men to their tents in the upland. The men told the commander's father about his son's courage. About his bravery, about how he crept behind the lines of the enemy and killed two of them with his own hands. He threw his *patu* over their heads, drew his dagger and slit their throats, with a quick cut.

From now on you are a real commander, his father had said, had embraced his son and sent him off to get the girl who had been promised him. A man is only a real man when he has a wife. A wife who will give him first one son, then many more. The commander's father gave his son a bundle of banknotes, gleaming and glittering fabrics, a horse, a rifle and so many other presents for the bride and her father that people whispered behind their hands, is she worth all that?

Ride off and get the girl, the commander's father said. Her name is Daria.

Daria. The boy's body twitches as if a shot hits him.

For four days and four nights he rides from his own upland plain to the one where his bride lives. The young commander, his men and his father put on their finest clothes and sit, with their weapons, with Daria's father, his men and their weapons in the meadow some way away from the tent where Daria waits. The men talk about the war, enemies and friends, allies and neighbours, about this and that, but not about Daria, her price and the wedding that is soon to be. The women of the family sit in the tent and observe the girl.

The hours come and go. The men talk and talk. The women talk and talk. They come out and say, Daria is beautiful. More beautiful than anyone else in the world. She is like a flower. As fresh as the first snow on the peaks of the mountains in the Hindu Kush. She is an angel. Her name does not lie, she is like the bubbling source of the stream that springs from the rocks in the mountains. The women say she will bear our young commander healthy sons. The young commander's mouth fills with water. His heart becomes a hundred hearts. A hundred hearts that want to burst through his chest.

For the young commander's father the matter is decided. Daria is the right girl for his son. The young commander wants to wait no longer, he wants to see his bride, to touch her, possess her, to make the girl a woman.

It is not wise, the commander's father says, to ask for the

bride's hand immediately after your first visit and your first discussions. It is not clever to show haste with such business. It raises the price of the bride. The bride's family should not think the bridegroom's father is in a hurry to marry his son. The bride's family might think this girl is the bridegroom's only choice.

I have no other choice, says the young commander.

The girl's family might think there is something wrong with you. They might think you lack something.

I lack nothing, says the young commander.

His men laugh, hold their bellies, slap their thighs.

Again the young commander says, I lack nothing.

You have not spent a night with a woman yet. You will see whether you lack something, say the men, and laugh louder and louder.

The young commander's father does not laugh.

The men fall silent.

In the evening the women of the family and the young commander's mother return to the tent to beautiful Daria and her mother. The young commander's father, his son and his men go to Daria's father, ask him to give his daughter to the young commander. The men talk, negotiate the price for the bride, ask questions, give answers, say But, say No, say Yes. The young commander sits and waits, waits and sits. He wants his Daria. Now. The poor young commander is ill, he is feverish. Blood rushes to his head. All the stories he carries within himself lose their beginning, lose their end. His men sit there, see their young commander, nudge one another, laugh. One of the men leans over to him, speaks quietly behind his hand so that only his new leader can hear it. Soon it will be time. It will not be long before you stand before your beautiful bride.

Little pearls of water appear on the brow of the young commander, water runs down his back. The young commander wants his sea-wife, he wants to touch her. His Daria, who is like the cool water, like the quiet splashing of the streams that spring from the rocks up in the mountains and turn into wild rivers down in the valleys. Rivers that drag everything and everyone along with them. His Daria; the river he will dive, plunge, disappear into.

Son, says his father. What is wrong with you? Move. Your bride is waiting.

The women beat their drums, clap their hands, trill their tongues, sing. The men rise to their feet, support their new leader, lead him to his bride's tent, push him in and wait outside.

The young commander sits next to his Daria. The scarf on her head slips, reveals her face. The commander does what is forbidden and looks into her eyes. The mullah sits in front of Daria and the young commander, recites verses from the Koran, sings, rocks his body back and forth, asks a thousand and one questions. The poor young commander sees and hears nothing of all the mullah is saying, doing and not doing. All the poor young commander knows is that he will soon possess the creature beneath the scarf.

When he is finally alone with his Daria, finally takes the scarf from her head, looks into her eyes, finally sees her smile, talks to her, when all this and everything else is finally permitted, the commander says something he had never intended to say. He says, I am afraid of you. I am afraid of drowning. I will drown in you, I will be dead and you will be alone.

Daria laughs, lifts her eyes, looks her commander openly

in the eyes and says, if you die because you have drowned in me, then I will not be alone.

The commander says nothing.

Daria's words sound like the gurgling of a stream. If you drown in me I will not be alone, for then you and I will be one.

The commander touches his Daria's hand as though her fingers were the feet of a butterfly. A butterfly that settles on his hand, beats its wings and flies off again.

Summer comes and goes. Winter comes and goes.

The commander was telling the truth. He sinks, he drowns in his Daria. Sometimes he sinks for ever. Sometimes he reappears again.

The commander does what is forbidden, he stays in the tent and waits for his Daria to pull his son out of her body. If people knew about it, they would despise both of them. People would talk behind their backs, call Daria a bad woman because she did not send her husband out. Daria knows that she is heaping blame upon herself.

The commander's body trembles, his head is heavy, his heart races, his skin is hot. Pictures and stories run back and forth in his head, play with his senses, try to drive him out of his mind. He wants to stop chewing the piece of bread, he wants to creep to his Daria, embrace her from behind, pull her firmly to him, press her to his chest, feel her back against him.

When is he finally going to come? he asks.

Daria wants to answer, she wants to tell her husband not to worry, wants to tell him that he is a man, that he must be strong. She wants to say, God is great, he will provide. The words are ready in her head, she closes her eyes so as not to lose the words. Daria loses the words. Heaven and earth swap places. Finally Daria feels beneath her fingers the damp little face of her son, the son she has carried in her belly throughout half the summer, the whole of the winter and the beginning of spring. Slowly, as though she is waking from deep sleep, life enters the young woman's body.

And what will you do if it is not a son?

The commander sits up, says, all the firstborn in my family are sons. Only if it is a son does it have the right to live.

Daria groans. Give me a piece of wood.

The commander leaps to his feet. A piece of wood? What for?

In the name of God. Don't ask, says Daria. I need it to bite on it.

The commander can hit the enemy right between the eyes from a long way off, but now he cannot even find a single clear thought. All she wants is a piece of wood, but the commander stumbles around the tent, hits himself on the head, hopes that his Daria will not see his impotence.

Daria sees everything. His impotence. His helplessness. Come here, she says, pulls her commander down on the floor, pushes him behind her, takes his hand, places it on her fat belly, says, push. Daria's breath grows calmer, her body relaxes. The commander kisses the pearls of sweat from the back of his Daria's neck, licks his lips. One last time she bends over, reaches beneath her belly, breathes violently, utters one final liberating, suffocated scream, pulls the child out of her body, holds the wrinkled, slimy, blood-covered being in her hands. The child pulls its legs up to its parchment-skinned belly, waves its arms around, puts its tiny hands in its mouth, shivers. Daria grabs the sickle, plunges it in the boiling water. With a quiet *be-isme-Allah* on her lips she parts the umbilical cord, knots around it the thread that she has pulled from the brightly coloured fabric of her dress. Daria wipes the blood from the skin of the newborn, wraps it in the white muslin. Did you see? she asks. It is only a girl.

The commander is silent.

His son is a girl.

A DECISION

The afterbirth falls from Daria's body with a quiet slap. The commander gets up, puts on his colourfully embroidered boots, puts his gun over his shoulder and leaves the tent. Outside he looks into the sky, wipes tears from his eyes, thanks God that his Daria has not seen them.

Two big birds are hovering in the sky. The commander narrows his eyes to slits, puts his gun to his shoulder, cocks it, aims. Inside the tent Daria hears the dry click of the rifle. Quietly, so quietly that only the water and her newborn can hear it, she says, he wanted a son, now he has tears in his eyes. Don't worry, says Daria, more to herself than to her daughter. He won't fire.

The commander follows the birds through the sights of his rifle until he cannot see them any more, until they have disappeared behind the peak of the mountain. Later he will say, the birds owe their lives to your birth. What he will not say to his child is, I would not have had tears in my eyes if you had been a boy.

The commander swings on to the back of his stallion, gallops away, towards the mountains. His mountains.

Where he is closest to heaven and his God. He urges on his stallion until it snorts loudly, its long mane blows in the wind like a flag, its hoofs thunder as though it were trying to ram them into the earth, until none of its four legs touches the earth. The tents of the other nomads, their animals, the nomad children, bushes, rocks, the stream – everything blurs together. The world is a bright mixture of colours and the thundering of the hooves, the stallion's snorting, the commander's breath. He flies past the cries of the men and boys. *Salam. Komandan. Zende bashi. Koja miri?* Greetings. Commander. Long may you live. Where are you going?

The commander does not reply, does not want the people to see his tears. He bends low over the neck of his stallion, claws his fingers into its mane. The commander and his stallion cleave together, become one. Half human, half animal.

The commander gallops until he reaches the foot of the highest mountain at the other end of the plain. Where the upland starts and finishes.

The people down in the village, in the valley, the ones who know more about God and the world than the people up here in the mountains, say that the mountains surrounding and protecting the upland plain are seven thousand metres high. They say the valley is four thousand metres high. The commander knows neither how much seven thousand metres is, nor four thousand metres, he knows only that these mountains are the highest he has ever climbed, the most beautiful he has ever seen. The people from the village and the south of the country call the commander and his people *kuchi*, mountain folk. Stupid mountain folk. The commander knows that he does not know much about the world, he has not seen much of it. But he knows that this piece of earth, his homeland, was made by God. People say that the commander and his clan are dangerous, they belong to the Hazara people. They are savages, they know neither law nor reason, friend nor enemy.

We can fight, says the commander. Being able to fight is also a kind of knowledge. If we were stupid, the enemy would have come to our highlands long ago and attacked us, plundered us, robbed our possessions, our tents and our animals, carried off our wives and daughters, raped them and taken the honour of our men. Our knowledge is enough for us, says the commander. It is the knowledge that makes me ruler over the upland and keeps my people safe.

All that the commander knows, all that his father and his father's fathers knew before him, is knowledge that can only be passed on to the first child, who must be a son. It is the knowledge which is locked in the rock of the commander and his father's fathers.

At the foot of the highest mountain stands the flat plate of rock on a stone plinth. The rock on which the commander sits, lies, dozes in the sun, sleeps at night when he travels through the mountains. It is his rock. The one that no one else may ever step upon.

This is the rock of God, his father said when the commander was still a little boy. It is a holy rock, it is the good lord's gift to men like you and me. Men who are born the first child, the first son. Firstborn sons of firstborn sons. Sons like you and me, like my father and our fathers' fathers. The commander's father spoke quietly. Because what he has to say is important. We have all derived our strength, our might, our knowledge from this rock. It is thanks to this rock that you and I and all our fathers' fathers have ruled over our upland plain. It is thanks to it alone that we cannot be conquered. Since the lord God has given me life, my father brought me here. Since my father fell in the war and became a martyr, a *shahid*, since he left me behind in this cruel yet not-cruel world, this place has belonged to me. And now, my son, this rock shall belong to you. And you too will bring your first child here, a son that God will give you, and you will instruct him in the truths of the world and life. You and your son will also bring honour to our name and rule the upland plain and the people who live in it. The rock is the gateway to this and all other worlds. The ones that exist and the ones that do not exist. All that your eye must see and wants to see, you can see from up here.

That isn't true, said the little boy, contradicting his father. That isn't true, I can't see the people in their tents, or the ones in the valley and the rest of the world.

Be patient, the commander's father replied. You will see. Close your eyes and trust the rock and its divine power. It will let you see whatever you wish to see, and what you do not wish to see you will see also. The father knelt before his son, gripped him by the arms and said, you can see it already, you just don't know it yet.

Many years came and went. The commander sat on his rock, his eyes closed, waiting, but all that he saw was the bare stones and rocks around him, the blue sky above him, the birds in it and the many mountains and valleys.

Some people say that since the commander has been going up to his rock he has become blessed. They say the commander carries the power of the holy rock within him. He has killed many men and freed them from their wicked existence, many of his soldiers have found a hero's death and become *shahid*. The spirits of all these dead come to him on his rock, speak to him and tell him all that they see and know. That is the reason for all the commander's strength and power.

Daria says the commander is neither blessed, nor do the dead speak to him.

The commander himself is content with all of this talk, both kind and not-kind. He says the more people talk about a man the more important he is.

The people talk about the young warrior's courage and bravery. They talk about the way he protects them and their families, just as his father and his father's fathers did before him. He keeps war far from his people. No one knows how many Russians, Taliban and other enemies of his homeland he has killed, but they all know there were many of them. Very many. Both women and men sit around the fire in their tents and say, it is only thanks to the commander that we need not suffer hunger, that we live a life in peace and calm, even when war rages everywhere else in our homeland.

The commander stands there, looks into the distance, knows that everything is as it always is. Knows also everything is different from the way it always is. Now, as always, the people will talk about him. They will say that the commander's first child is not a son. They will say his son is a girl. They will say the commander is not a man. Not a real man.

The commander did not ask his father what would happen if anyone but himself and his son were to step upon the rock. He knows the answer. A disaster would come. A huge disaster. The commander has never broken the law of the rock, but the huge disaster still came. The first child that his wife has pulled out of her body for him turned out to be a girl.

His Daria knows too, that it was her duty to pull a son out of her body as her commander's first child. She squats by her fire, watches the bubbles jumping out of the pot and landing in the flames. Now he will despise me, Daria says to the simmering water. I have lost my worth.

Had she pulled a son out of her body, the commander would have been proud of her and his child. Everyone could have seen it, the commander is a real man, because his first child is a son. The commander would not have ridden to his rock, would have stayed in the tent with his son and his wife, would have thanked her, honoured and respected her, would have given her presents, slaughtered a lamb and given a feast to celebrate the birth of his first son.

What he will do instead, Daria does not know. She knows men who have denied their daughter, who have taken a second wife and impregnated her in the hope that the new wife will pull a son out of her body. In the hope that people will not talk behind his back, saying that so-and-so is not man enough to father a son. A man is only a real man when he has fathered a son. Daria knows women who for this reason have been beaten and driven away by their husbands. She knows women who have no teeth in their mouths. Their husbands knocked them out, because instead of sons they pulled only girls out of their bodies. Daria has asked the older women why the men had knocked their wives' teeth out. Because a woman who does not bear her husband a son, the older women said, is not a woman. Because her husband can no longer use her as a woman. Daria did not understand. A wife who cannot be used as a woman can use her mouth just as well to satisfy her husband's desire, the women said, looked around, spoke quietly. The teeth of a woman get in the way when the husband satisfies his desire in her mouth.

Daria swallows down tears, catches a bubble that jumps from the pot, saves it from landing in the fire and dying there. God, Merciful, says Daria. Stand by me and my daughter.

Daria looks at the heavy, dark roof of her felt tent, sees the newborn lambs huddling against one another on the floor, sees the earth next to the hole she has dug, sees the afterbirth that she should have carried outside long ago, sees the flies that have gathered on it, feeding from it. Daria sees the sickle she used to part the cord, picks it up and hangs it over the central wooden post that holds up the felt roof. Daria bends over her daughter in the little hammock, looks at her, says, I wish instead of being born a girl you had been born dead.

The girl furrows her brow and looks as though she is thinking about what the big words of the woman bent over her might mean. As though she knows the mother's words mean nothing good.

Without smiling, without emotion, without love, Daria strokes her daughter's head, looks at her and says, now that you turned out to be a girl, God alone knows what your father will do with you and me.

Daria takes her child in her arm, takes the sickle from the post, looks at her daughter, says nothing. Her daughter closes her eyes, opens them again, stretches out her arm, with her fingers touches her mother's face. It is a small touch, as though a butterfly sits on Daria's face, beats its wings and instantly flies away again. It is a small, big touch that takes all significance from Daria's fear, doubts, every thought. It takes significance from everything and everyone. A touch that turns Daria's heart to paper and tears it. With a rip. A quiet rip, so as not to startle the child.

Daria sees the sickle in her hand, does not know why she is holding it, throws it. It lands on the afterbirth in the hole with a faint slap, so that the flies are startled and buzz away.

A gentle, light breeze floats through the tent, gives Daria wings. She leaves her body behind, rises up, dips down into a stream, rises high up to where only the biggest and strongest of all birds fly. Neither yesterday nor tomorrow are important. Life is right as it is.

Now that I have you, says Daria, what do I care for the people and the things they say? What do I care for the rock? Let him go to his rock as often as he will. Be without sorrow, Daria says gently, in a soft voice. In a voice that only her daughter knows.

Daria puts her words and thoughts on the wings that the wind has brought her, sends them up to the mountain, to the rock, to her commander.

The commander knows that until now the first child, who has always been a son, has taken the place of his father. Until now. But after him, when he himself no longer comes here, who will come to the rock? His daughter? A girl? A woman?

He covers his face with his hands. I should blow you up, says the commander to his rock, because there is no one else he can say it to. The commander shrugs his shoulders. My Daria speaks to the water, I speak to the rock, he says, presses his face to the stone, dozes off, dreams. First of his

Daria, then of other women. Women who do not belong to any other man. Women he does not know. Women who do not exist. Not in the real world, only in the commander's head. Fear rushes through his body, opening his eyes wide. Fear that makes his head spin, fear that moves like a snake. Fast and skilful it moves its long, smooth body silently among the sand of the desert, the stones and rocks. The fear-snake creeps into his blood, moves through his veins and muscles.

In the end these dreams are the very reason why the good Lord did not give me a son, but only a daughter, the commander says. For it is a sin to think of strange women. Then it is my fault that my firstborn has turned out to be a girl.

The commander knew the day would come when the Lord would punish him for his pictures of women. He had feared that day, had tried to forget his fear, had forgotten it. Because winter and summer came and went, but God did not send his punishment, the commander assumed it had been forgiven. Because, after all, he had done so much good. Never resting, he had fought for the Prophet, for the Koran, for the true Islam. He had freed his homeland, had slit his enemy's throat.

The commander thinks and thinks. He broods and asks questions. But he receives no answer. He grabs his rifle, jumps from the rock, swings on to the back of his horse, gallops off, shoves his heels into his stallion's belly, urging it on until there is white foam at its mouth, until its hide becomes warm and damp.

Long before Daria hears the stallion's hooves, she whispers in her daughter's tiny ear, your father's coming. He won't drive you away, he just doesn't know it yet.

The commander comes into his tent. Give me my child, he says. He is not asking his Daria. It is an order.

What do you want with her? asks Daria.

It is my child, I can do with it what I want, he says.

You can, says Daria, handing the commander his daughter.

The commander is taking his child in his big hands, he is just about to leave the tent with her, he does not know why he has taken her, what he is going to do with her, when the little girl's dark eyes gleam like the commander's rock. She yawns, stretches out her tiny hand, the skin of her fingers is so transparent that the commander can see her fragile bones. The girl grips her father's thumb. That is all she does. She holds the thumb, her eyes fall shut, she breathes calmly, grows heavy, falls into a calm and deep sleep.

Samira, says the commander, quietly, lest he wake his child. Let that be your name. Samira.

Daria puts wood in the warm embers, fans the fire, says, Samira. That means heart, inner wealth.

But Samira also means secret, says the commander. We will give her the name Samira, we will call her Samir, he says, lowers his eyes, does not look at Daria, says, so that people think you have given me a son.

Daria looks at her commander, says, so that people think I have given you a son. Then Daria says nothing more.

All the rest of the night and all the next day Daria does not say a single word, the commander only lets his child out of his hands when it wants its mother's breast. Only at the end of that long day does Daria speak again. In a voice that is calm and gentle. She says, Samir is a pretty name. Then she laughs briefly. It is a laugh that she quickly loses again. Daria looks the commander in the eyes and says, give me my girl-son, I miss him. The commander obeys, puts his child in its mother's arms and goes to leave the tent.

Don't go, says Daria, I miss you too. Come and lie with us. We want to sleep.

An Amulet

That's him, the people say when the commander sits his daughter-son on the saddle in front of him and rides past them. That's the commander and his son Samir.

Four summers and four winters have come and gone since Samira's birth. Something has happened that the commander is unable to understand. Something he has not wanted. He is full of unhappiness because his little Samir, although he is not a real boy, has conquered his father's heart, and meanwhile has become so important, so much a part of his life that the commander can no longer imagine living without him.

Daria says, take a new wife who can give you a son.

The commander says, perhaps I will.

Daria knows it, the commander knows it. The rock's law and that of his fathers' fathers say his firstborn child must be a son. This means the commander would have to find a way to get rid of his Samir.

How am I supposed to do that? asks the commander.

Daria is silent.

Let us leave things as they are, says the commander, and see what happens.

So summer and winter come and go, and Samira is and remains her father's only child.

The commander knows that he will be able to bend and break his Samir, but he will not be able to make a boy of him. Not a real boy. He knows that he can cheat and lie to human beings, but not his God and the rock, he knows that his father and all his father's fathers have had sons as their first child, he knows that his first child would only have had the right to live if it had been a son. The commander knows all of this, he just cannot find a way out

Another summer and winter comes and goes without the commander making a decision. He leaves everything as it is and hopes that God will show him the right way.

In the winters, when the cold and snow come into the mountains of the Hindu Kush, he leads his people to the warm South. Then when the snow goes again, he brings them back to the upland. Whenever he does not have to go to war to protect his people and his high plain, whenever he does not spend the night on the rock to absorb its power and wisdom, whenever he is not down in the village to sell a sheep, skins or anything else, or to trade for salt or flour or whatever, the commander spends all his time with his Samir, rides across the plain with him, takes him along into the mountains to hunt, to play *buzkashi*.

Watch me, he says to his daughter-son, watch carefully. The commander squats in the stream, does not move, stares into the water, waits for the fishes. As soon as one has come close enough, he deals it a blow with the flat of his hand and slings the fish from the water on to the shore. The fish lies on the ground, twitches and dances. The commander grabs it by the tail, strikes its head on a stone and lays it next to the others in a beautiful row.

I want them to dance, shouts Samira, cries and shrieks, throws the fishes one after the other back into the water, screams, you shall come back to life.

The commander grabs his Samir, brings him back to the shore, says, watch me.

Samira pulls away, kicks her father, hits him, spits at him.

The commander grabs his daughter-son by the shoulders, says, we need the fishes because we want to eat them. People kill animals so that they do not die themselves. That is how God wills it.

I don't care what God wills, Samira yells, throws stones at her father, beats him with the stick, throws herself on the ground, pulls out grass, throws it in the air and on to herself, claws in the sand with her hands, throws it in the air and on to herself as well. She rages and makes so much noise that the people come to the shore to see what all the shouting is for.

Daria comes, walks past her raging child without looking at it, walks past her helpless commander without looking at him, climbs into the stream, collects the dead fishes floating on the surface of the water in her dress, brings them to the shore, lines them up. Beautifully in order, one next to another, then she smiles, looks first at her commander, then at her daughter and says, those are beautiful fishes.

But they are not dancing any more, shouts Samira and starts crying. A quiet crying that turns hearts to paper and tears them apart.

It's good that they have stopped dancing, says Daria. She sits down and spreads her arms, waiting for her child to come to her.

Samira puts her arm around her mother's neck, leans her body against her, sniffs back the tears in her nose, asks, why is it good?

Because we want to eat the fishes, says Daria.

Samira nods, says, I know. She points at her father. The one there said so.

Then you know why it is good that they have stopped dancing and why they have to be dead, says Daria.

No, I don't know that, says Samira.

Do you not want to catch fish yourself? asks Daria.

Samira nods. I want to catch them, but I don't want them to be dead.

But they have to be dead, says Daria in a voice full of patience and reason. Reason that only the mother has. How can I put them on the spit and hang them over the fire if they are still alive, twitching and dancing?

Samira shrugs her shoulders. *Man che midanam.*

Khob, fine, says Daria. We have to kill them because otherwise we will not get them on the spit and will not be able to hang them over the fire and eat them.

Khob, says the child. It sounds like her mother's *khob*. *Khob*. Let me go. I must catch fish, I must kill them so that you can put them on the spit and we can eat them.

Bass and *khalass*. Daria leaves hold of her child, goes back to her tent.

The commander stands there and does not know how Daria has, once again, managed to make his child understand her. He walks after his Daria. The child follows you, he says. Not me.

Daria sits by her fire, pulls the bread out of the oven, looks at her commander. She would much rather follow you than me, Daria says. Look at her, she is sitting by the stream and trying to catch fish. She wants to be like you. Big, strong and invincible.

The commander is silent. Says nothing. Just stands there, leaves the tent, swings on to the back of his stallion, rides back to the stream.

Samira crouches in the stream, sees nothing and no one, is enchanted, enthralled, stares into the water. She needs all her little-girl strength not to be pulled away by the current. With one hand she holds on to a branch sticking into the water, the other she holds over the stream to strike the first fish that comes near her. Around her it is wriggling with fish. Small ones and big ones. They swim close to Samira, so close as if they wanted to nibble her foot. As soon as Samira prepares to make a grab for them or sling them out of the water, they make a rapid movement and disappear. Samira and the fishes are playing a game. The fishes enjoy their game with the human child, they know that it is not going to be dangerous for them.

Samira and the fishes are so engaged in their game that they do not notice the big bird that circles high above in the blue sky, and comes lower and lower. Samira is just whacking the water uselessly again, a fish is just escaping her, when the big bird screeches, draws back its wings, plunges from the sky, snaps the fat fish right out of the water next to Samira and disappears back into the sky with it.

Samira beats the water, fishes a stone from the bed of the stream, throws it after the bird, watches it disappear and curses when behind her the loud hooves of her father's enormous stallion come stamping noisily through the water. Samira is neither frightened of the bird, nor is she startled by the thundering of the hooves, neither is she afraid of the water that the enormous animal throws up and wets her with from head to toe. Samira turns round to the stallion, spreads her arms and her father, while riding, leans down and pulls her up to him on the back of the horse, as though he were playing the game of *buzkashi*, as though she were the sheep that he must wrestle from his opponents, as though she were a sack of onions. He hoists his daughter into the air, puts her on the saddle in front of him, shoves his heels into his horse's belly and rides through the stream towards the big meadow where his own tent and the tents of the other *kuchi* stand.

Samira likes it when the water splashes up, when the wind flies through her hair, when she has to close her eyes lest they fill with tears. She likes riding up and down the plain with her father, fast as the wind. She likes it when he laughs, because she cries happily, faster, faster, make him fly. I want to fly.

It's getting dark, says the commander, and rides back to the tent with his Samir, leaps from the horse and catches his daughter-son, who drops into his arms. The commander has barely put his child on the floor when Samira runs to the chickens that Daria has already shut up under their baskets for the night. Samira lifts up one of the baskets, frees the chicken beneath it, laughs, claps her hands. Daria grabs Samira by the arm and goes to drag her into the tent.

Let him be, the commander says. He grabs his Samir by the other arm, says, go. Get it.

Daria lets go of her child.

Samira does what her father has said, runs after the chicken with arms outstretched and tries to catch it. The chicken cackles loudly, beats its wings, ruffles up its feathers, pecks at Samira.

My son is no way inferior to the other boys, the commander says to himself, because there is no one else he can say it to. The commander is just saying, in fact he even outdoes them in many things, when Samira trips and falls. Without hesitating she stands up again, pays no attention to her cracked knee and the blood, goes on chasing the chicken.

For God's sake tell her to stop it, says Daria. What does she want with the stupid chicken?

Leave him alone, says the commander, without looking at his wife.

Daria leaves her child alone.

Samira throws herself on the chicken, catches it, runs around with it, shrieks. The chicken cackles as if its life were at stake. It is not the first time that Samira chases a chicken, catches it and is then afraid of it, runs around the place, does not know what to do with it. The chicken pecks wildly around, at Samira's hand, her arm, her belly.

The commander laughs and says, a real boy who wants to master the game of *buzkashi* must start practising early.

I know, says Daria, a real boy must start early. A real boy.

The commander says nothing.

Daria takes off her scarf, shakes it out as though black thoughts from her head had collected in it. Since when is catching chickens the correct preparation for the game of *buzkashi*?

The commander says nothing.

Samira runs to her mother with the chicken, throws it into her arms. Pain does not count, Samira babbles her father's words without knowing what she is saying. I am training to be a good *buzkashi* player. I am invincible, she says, knowing neither what the game of *buzkashi* is nor that no one is invincible. Samira straightens her little body and says, defiantly, I am a real boy, and has no idea.

A bubble jumps from the pot, Daria catches it, saves it from dying in the fire, says, stupid bubble. I am frightened, says Daria. I fear the day when the fact that my daughter is a girl can no longer be hidden. People will call my commander a liar. He will lose his standing and his power, my child and I will lose his protection, the commander will leave me and my child, drive us away, or do something else with us.

At night Daria sees terrible sleep-images. The clothes are ripped from her daughter's body. Men spit at her, throw stones at her, beat her, take her by force, enter her and spill her blood. To regain their injured manly honour. Because it is not the business of a woman to be as strong as a man, to rise up and live the life of a man. Daria tells the commander about the cruel images that tear her nights apart.

The decision has been made, says the commander.

It is time to make a new decision, says Daria. What will you do the day your lie comes out?

Do not dare call me a liar, says the commander, slashes the air with his short *buzkashi* whip. He raises his hand, holds it in the air, does not strike, jumps on to his horse, rides off to his rock and only comes back when night has fallen, shakes and rocks his Daria until she wakes. It is your fault that the first child you pulled out of your body was not a real boy. It is your fault that I have no son that I can take with me to the rock. It is your fault that I shall no longer be ruler of the upland.

Daria says nothing.

You say it is time to make a new decision. Tell me what kind of decision that is to be.

Daria cannot see her commander's eyes in the darkness, but knows they are full of hate. She peels herself out of her blankets, goes out, squats outside the tent. The commander follows her, stares at his Daria for a long time before he says, I'm frightened.

You are right to be frightened.

The commander shrugs his shoulders. I did not ask you whether I was right to be frightened, I want you to tell me what to do.

How should I know? asks Daria. I only know that if you do not take your child up to the rock soon, people are going to ask questions. Your reputation and your honour are at stake.

The commander smashes his fist on the floor. Damn it, you do not understand. She is not a real boy. If her foot touches the rock, a great misfortune will happen.

You are right, says Daria. I do not understand. How can it be that a stone, a dead rock, has so much power over you?

Be quiet, says the commander in a voice filled with rage. Do not talk about things you do not understand.

Daria obeys and says nothing.

As soon as day breaks, she creeps from her tent, and goes to Bibi-jan, the old midwife, the wise woman, the saint. Peace be with you, she says, bends down, kisses the old woman's wrinkled hand.

Bibi-jan has already lived so many summers and winters under God's heaven that no one, not even she herself, knows how many. People believe her and trust her, follow her advice, want her to pull their children from the bodies of their wives. People come to her when they are sick, bring their half-dead children and their cattle to her. Bibi-jan is there when people marry and when they die. Before the men go off to war they come to her, let her touch them, bless them, comfort them, give them courage. Courage to kill. Courage to be killed.

What do you want? asks Bibi-jan.

Daria cannot utter a sound, is looking at her bare feet, does not know how to ask Bibi-jan for help without revealing her secret, when Bibi-jan says, I see, it's about your child.

Daria starts back, alarmed. Daria hears it clearly. Bibi-jan has not said, your son. She has said, your child.

You are worried about your child because your commander still has not taken it up to his rock, says Bibi-jan.

How do you know? asks Daria, and is afraid that Bibi-jan already knows the secret of Samira and Samir.

Because your commander is not the first man in his family not to have taken his child up on to the rock.

I did not know that, says Daria.

There's a lot you do not know, says Bibi-jan.

The rock is sacred, says Daria.

Bibi-jan spits, says, the men in your commander's family believe that and want people to believe that. Your commander believes he owes all his power and strength to the rock. The truth is your commander is mistaken. The rock and its laws do not bring only good fortune and favour to him and his family.

Daria says nothing.

You are not the first woman to have suffered as a result of that rock. That dead stone is a curse to many of the women and children in your commander's family. Bibi-jan rummages around in a bag, takes something out, spits in her hand, utters many strange words that Daria does not understand. The old woman looks at Daria. Until this day no woman has had the courage to do anything against the men's rock.

Daria swallows, does not know what to say, says nothing and thinks, thinks and says nothing, then she says, I will do it. Tell me what I am to do.

I knew you had courage, says Bibi-jan.

I have no courage, says Daria. I am frightened. I am only doing it because I cannot see any other way of protecting my own life and the life of my child.

That is a good decision, says Bibi-jan. Take this amulet, tie the *ta-vis* around your neck, it will give you strength and show you the right way to break the spell of the rock. After you have defeated the rock, tie the amulet around your Samir's neck and tell him it will protect him and destroy everyone and everything that seeks to harm him.

Daria holds the amulet in her hand. Very firmly.

But you should know, says Bibi-jan. This *ta-vis* has no strength or value if you do not believe in it. And you should also know that the ways of God are unfathomable.

I know, says Daria. God comes and goes whenever he wants. He does what he wants, he allows whatever he wants to happen.

Instead of going back to her tent, Daria goes to the stream, sits on the banks, dangles her feet in the cold water, plays with the stones in the bed of the stream, thinks and thinks and keeps looking at the amulet again and again. It is long and thin and no bigger than her thumbnail and it has four little holes. On one side it is white, like the flowers in the meadow. On the other dull as a bone. Pull a thread through the four holes, Bibi-jan said, be a warrior. Nothing will happen to you and your child.

Daria the warrior. Daria the victor. Daria with blame.

Daria with her Samira, who is Samir. Daria with a white *ta-vis*, with four small holes. One hole for God, one for herself, one for the child she has pulled out of her body, one for the children she did not pull out of her body. Daria sits by the stream, pulls a thread from her dress, draws it through the four small holes, ties the amulet around her neck. She gives a start when her commander appears behind her and asks, what are you doing here?

I am sitting, says Daria, amazed at the courage in her voice.

The commander too is so astonished by his Daria's new voice that he does not ask or say anything else. He squats beside her and throws stones into the water.

Bibi-jan said I was to be a warrior, Daria thinks, and says, who knows, maybe somewhere in the big wide world there are other fathers who bring up their daughters as sons.

What do you mean by that? asks the commander.

Who knows, says Daria. After all it could be that some of the men you have fought have been women.

The commander's breath quickens, blood rushes through his body, boils at the idea that his enemy might have had breasts.

I smell your desire, says Daria. But is your blood not becoming bitter, is it not boiling and rising to your head? Is it not giving you pain, making you ill at the thought of the shame and disgrace that might have fallen upon you?

What disgrace? asks the commander.

You, the great warrior and fighter may have fought a woman, you may have defeated a woman, says Daria.

Be quiet, says the commander.

Daria is quiet, touches her *ta-vis*, then is not quiet; she asks, what sort of victory is that? Victory over a woman is not a hero's victory. Victory over a woman is a coward's victory. Battle with a woman is a battle without decency or dignity.

The commander raises his hand, does not hold his hand in the air, strikes out.

Daria does not lower her eyes, stares him straight in the face.

It is your fault I hit you, says the commander.

God is witness, says Daria. If this child were not your child, you would take its father to account, you would insist on justice. You would put an end to this insult, this mockery and the shame it brings down upon the whole world of men who have faith.

The commander draws his short *buzkashi* whip from his boot, Daria leaps to her feet, says, she will never be like you. And do not dare strike me again.

You are my wife, says the commander. I can do what I want with you.

Do it then, says Daria. Then I will tell everyone that your son is a girl.

Then I will kill you, says the commander.

Daria draws the commander's knife from his belt, throws it at his feet, says, kill me. Go on. But it will do you no good.

The commander says nothing.

One death more or less, what difference does that make? asks Daria. None. None at all.

A SEDUCTION

It is a mild day in spring when Daria does it. The air is filled with the scent of fresh flowers, the birds are singing, and a gentle breeze is blowing. Daria stands barefoot in front of her commander, with her hair like pitch, like velvet, with her tattoo on her forehead, with her mouth that reminds the commander of a fresh peach. Daria has rubbed her body with rosewater, she is wearing her most ample and brightly coloured skirt, she has tied strips of cloth embroidered with shells and pearls, coins and bones around her neck and her belly.

God and Bibi-jan's *ta-vis* have shown Daria the way. If she can make the commander break the law of the rock, she will also persuade him to take his Samir up on to the rock. So Daria stands in front of her commander, made up, hair combed, with her jangling jewellery she twists and writhes and turns the poor commander's head.

At the end of all her jangling, twisting and writhing she opens her eyes, like two black butterflies about to fly away. Daria smiles, lays her hand on the commander's chest, looks at him with her black-rimmed almond eyes until the commander puts his hand on her hand. Then Daria says, you do want a son.

The commander wants to swallow, but cannot remember how. His chest glows beneath her hand, the rest of his body turns warm and hot. He simply stands there with that unfamiliar, beautiful burning in his chest, and no longer knows even whether he is awake or asleep, whether he is alive or dead.

The commander's other hand dangles limply by his side as though it does not belong to him. Daria takes his limp hand, gives him the reins of his horse and says, come.

Only now does the commander see that his stallion has been standing behind his Daria the whole time.

Take them, she says. We are going for a ride.

The commander wants to ask, where? Can not find the word. Instead he obeys, swings on to his horse, holds his hand out to Daria and pulls her up on the saddle in front of him. He sits there like a sack of onions, a big sack of onions. He does not pull the reins around, or shove his boot into the horse's side. Rather than asking where they are riding too, he sits there and feels his Daria's back, her hip.

She straightens up, shoves her bare feet into the horse's side, moves her body back and forth, presses her thigh against his male desire, which seethes now and intensifies all the while. The poor commander does not know why he is riding or where he is riding to. Only when he sees his rock glinting and gleaming in the distance does he find the words in his head and ask, where are we riding to?

To your rock, says Daria.

Why are we doing that? asks the commander

Because we are going to conceive your son there, says Daria, shoves her feet into the stallion's side one last time, leans her head against her commander's powerful chest and says nothing more.

The commander knows very well he should say it is not a woman's business to tell her husband what to do, everyone else but him is forbidden even to approach the rock, let alone go up on to it, and he should say that a son is no use to him now because his first child is not a son. But on this day, when everything is different from every other day, the commander says nothing of any of this. He dismounts from his horse, catches his Daria, embraces her, holds her. It is an embrace the like of which he has never known. Without knowing why, he kisses her beautiful throat, her shoulder, the nape of her neck, he does what is forbidden, he lifts her up into the air as though she were a sack of onions, and pushes her up on to his rock.

A thousand and one times Daria has imagined how it would be up here. She had secretly wished to sit on the rock and discover her husband's secrets. Now she is here, at last. At last Daria is sitting on the smooth, black, sun-warmed surface. A breeze, not cold, not warm, strokes her face, the sun casts its light on Daria, the air is gentle and soft. But Daria is trembling. She is breathing with difficulty. Her skin is cold. Little pearls of water appear on her forehead, water runs over her back, her chest, her belly. The nape of her neck is damp. Daria closes her eyes, supports herself on the rock so as not to fall, tries to calm herself. She opens her eyes, closes them again, cannot stop the spinning in her head. Daria has committed a sin, she has used her cunning to make her commander take her up on to the rock. Daria has guilt. Great guilt for which she will have to atone. Daria has done it for her child. But now she is here she realises how stupid of her it was to believe she was the warrior who could break the spell of the rock. Daria is full of fear, wants to leap into her commander's arms, wants to get back to the safety of her tent, to her fire and the water bubbles. But however much she might want to, she cannot. Daria is rigid. The rock has turned her to stone. She has become one with her commander's dead, immobile rock.

Slowly, very slowly, without her noticing, her body loses its hold, sinks forward until her chest touches the stone with a faint slap. She feels the sun's warmth on her back, she sees a passing angel squat on the edge of the rock, his hand outstretched, touch her amulet, beat his wings four times and fly inside her.

God has sent his angel, says Daria. He lives within me.

The commander says nothing, lies down on his back, pulls his Daria to him, embraces her, closes his eyes and inhales her fragrance.

You are breaking the sacred law of the rock, says Daria.

The commander says nothing.

Aren't you afraid of the punishment? asks Daria.

The commander says nothing.

May God grant that you do not blame me for breaking the law, says Daria, and knows he is doing that already.

Daria moves away from her commander, turns her back on him, touches her amulet, whispers, protect me. The angel who lives within her beats his wings. The commander puts his arms around her, draws her to him, inhales the fragrance of her hair, hoists up her skirts, opens his *shalvar*, makes love to her as he has never made love to her before and never will again.

God is great, the commander says into the darkness, he will provide.

It is so, says Daria. He will show you a way to pass on the

knowledge that is enclosed within the rock of your father and your father's fathers to your child.

The days become birds, flock together and fly away.

Daria has broken the spell of the rock. She ties the amulet to her child's neck and says, it will protect you and destroy anything and anyone that tries to do you harm.

Daria sits kneading the dough, not looking at her commander, tears pieces off the dough, and rolls it into round balls between her hands. It is time for you to take him up on to your rock.

In the name of God, says the commander in a voice filled with revulsion. No one but me and my son is permitted ever to walk upon the rock. The commander picks up a stone, throws it, hits nothing and nobody.

You have broken the sacred law of your rock once before, says Daria, when you took me up there. So you can break it again and take your Samir along, says Daria, and knows that God and the *ta-vis* will provide, knows that the commander will do it.

It was not my fault, says the commander. You made me do it.

It was God's will, he sent his angel, says Daria.

It is not God's fault, says the commander.

A Shot

Daria, with her child on her arm, stands in front of the tent and does not know why it is as it is, but knows as surely as if she had been there that a shot has been fired.

It is war. Every day that God gives to the people in her homeland, shots are fired, missiles fly, bombs explode. Poor Daria, why are you so concerned about that one shot? Have you forgotten? Men kill men.

They kill mothers, fathers, daughters, sons. So many that no one has a tear left for them. Men set fire to houses, huts and tents. So many that no one wants to know how many. Houses with and without people in them, with children, women and men in them.

Men rape a thousand and one women. Drag them away, slit bellies open, sever heads from necks with one quick cut. Men loot, rob, demand toll-money. Legs tear off, hands are hacked off, arms are crushed. Blood sticks to the hands of men.

Daria sees the war, although it is far away. Her sleep-images are full of it. Are full of blood. Before he went back to war, Daria told the commander about her sleep-images.

Someone has collected all the blood in my pots and bowls, it has flowed out of our tent, has stained the floor, the stream and all the waters in our homeland red. God gives us blood-days. For so many summers and winters that I do not know how many.

Twenty-five, says the commander.

That is twenty-five too many, says Daria.

The blood of war is smeared over Daria's heart, her ears are full of the cries of war, she has the taste of war on her tongue.

How do I know about that one shot? Daria asks her child, because there is no one else there for her to ask.

The gunman took his time, shouldered his rifle, calmed his breath, took aim, fired. The shot flew. Every shot lands somewhere. In a leg, an arm, a head, a heart. This shot too landed somewhere. In the commander. In his testicle. Blood flowed. The commander's blood.

You are lucky, say the men who lay the commander on the ground in front of the tent. They are the men who go to the front, to the war, and fight under his command.

What are they fighting for? They do not know any more.

You are lucky he is alive, say the fighting men.

I am lucky, says Daria.

The commander's clothes are full of blood. His eyes are closed. There is hardly any life left in his body. He is still.

Bibi-jan watches with Daria over the half-dead man. Daria dips a cloth into her simmering water, puts herbs in it, lays them on the wound. On the testicle he no longer has. She drips water into his mouth, washes him, rubs oil into his otherwise strong and healthy body. Daria talks to him and knows that he hears her. Your son is with the horses, plays with them, lies with them in the meadow, climbs over their bodies, dozes in the sun. Daria knows that if the commander were awake he would say, that is impossible. Horses do not lie down, they do not let children crawl on them.

Daria talks and talks, knows he hears her. When you have woken up again, she says, you will take your son up on to the rock and instruct him in all the secrets. Daria knows that now the commander has lost his manhood, he will do it.

The commander sleeps and sleeps. Day and night. Many days, many nights. Deeper and heavier than he has ever slept before.

He will wake up, she says to her child.

Samira climbs around on the half-dead man, plays with his beard, lies on his chest, goes to sleep on him, wakes up, talks to him. Babbles all day, talks about the horses she lies with in the meadow. I am full of courage, I put my hand into your stallion's mouth. Wake him up, she says to her mother. I don't want him to sleep.

He will wake up, says Daria.

He has turned into a fish. He is dead, says the child.

No, says Daria. He is not dead.

Daria speaks the truth.

The commander wakes up, opens his eyes, says, horses do not lie on the ground. Horses do not let a child crawl around on them.

Daria knows better.

The commander sees his child, sees his wife, turns away, weeps. Tears that he does not swallow down. Tears he wants Daria and his child to see. The commander knows what has happened.

A Discovery

A little amulet with four holes, Samira and Samir, Daria with guilt, the commander, with a Nothing instead of testicles and manhood, spend the summer in the upland of the Hindu Kush.

The sack of wheat is almost empty. The bag of salt has been empty for a long time. The box of tea is no longer full. The sugar has been used up. The cloth in which the commander kept his money is empty. Some days Samira's belly is empty.

No one knows why, but the war is quiet. The Taliban are fighting in the north of the country. They have conquered another city. The cruel ruler betrayed his people. Switched sides again, went over to the Taliban. Along with them he rounded up seven thousand and more people in front of their huts and slaughtered them.

Yakolang is burning.

The Taliban barricade the houses and set them alight, people are burned alive. Their blood is on the hands of the Taliban, the hands of the ruler and his men. The hands of the men who are paying him.

For ever and into all eternity.

This time it is not Daria's fault.

Why is it always men? asks Daria.

The commander shrugs.

The warlord has switched sides once again, has gone over to the side of the other men who were once his allies, then became his enemies, now they are his friends again.

He has seven thousand Taliban and more slaughtered.

Their blood too, is on the hands of the warlord and the men who pay him.

For ever and into all eternity. No one knows why.

Only one thing they know. It is always men.

Some of them pay. Others kill.

The dead are children. Women. Old men. Cripples. Teachers. Peasants. People with one leg. People with one arm. People with reason. People without reason.

The cruel ruler flees.

Some people say, perhaps he is dead.

Other people say, if only he was. Dead.

If only they were all dead. The murderers of the dead.

Samira knows nothing of killing and killers, of war and battles. Samira knows only that this summer her father did not go to war. Her father is with her. With his daughter-son.

Samir. Come. The commander speaks quietly, because what he has to say is important. Because Samir alone is to hear it.

Before the sun casts its first light and its first warmth over the mountain, the commander whispers into the sleeping ear of his child. Whispered words are secret words, they are important. Important father-whispered words.

Every morning the same thing. The father and his child stand outside, in the remaining darkness and the cold of night, to wake the sun. The commander takes his girl-son on his arm, wraps himself and his child in his *patu*, hugs the child close.

Shut your eyes, says Samira. Do not worry, I have called the sun, it will come. The commander's heart turns to paper and tears.

Daria does not wait for the sun, sees her daughter and her commander, sits by the oven-hole in the floor, lights the fire. Father and daughter call to the sun. Daria calls to the fire.

Daria is lucky.

The other *kuchi* women have no oven-hole in the floor of their tent. The other women's husbands are not as good to them as the commander is to his Daria.

Daria is lucky. She talks to the water in her pot and catches the bubbles.

She sat behind her commander and watched as he built the oven for her. The commander dug out the hole, stamped down the soil and said, so that you will be comfortable.

So that the bread I bake for you tastes better, Daria said.

The fire burns brightly, warming the tent, the smell of baking dough settles on everything and everyone, the commander says, it looks like the sun. As though you had caught the sun in your oven.

Catching the sun is what you and your Samir do, says Daria.

The father and his child stand in front of the tent, eyes closed, wait for the sun. Here it comes, says Samira.

Each time she is enthralled once again, is enraptured by the play of the sun, its light and its warmth. Samira's breath is quick, her heart pounds.

Can you feel it? asks the commander.

Yes, whispers the child.

What do you feel?

The beginning of the sun.

Gently, carefully the sun casts a faint light over the mountains and announces its arrival. It colours the dark sky orange, and shows a thin strip of itself.

I can hear it, says the child.

What can you hear? asks her father.

Its crackling. Its breath.

What you hear is the wood waking from its sleep. It's the rocks, the mountain, the stones absorbing the warmth of the sun, the blades of grass slowly straightening, the flowers opening their blossoms. What you hear is the people in the other tents starting their day, the horses, sheep, goats, camels shaking their bones.

Samira looks at her father, listens to her father's words as though they were a fairy-tale from the *Thousand and One Nights*. Later Samira will go to the stream, gather the other children around her and repeat everything word for word. She will ask the same questions, give the same answers.

She will speak like her father, pause between her words as he does, look the children in the eyes as her father looks her in the eyes. She will raise and lower her hands, she will twist and turn them as he does. Like him, she will lower her head, think, only then will she speak.

The other children love and hate listening to Samira. No one can tell stories as beautifully as she can. The people in her stories are alive, they breathe, weep and laugh. Samira tells them about wood waking up, and herself becomes wood.

The wood is speaking, says Samira.

You're lying, the children cry. Wood doesn't sleep and it doesn't speak, and it isn't true that you can hear the grass straightening.

You're stupid, says Samira. You know nothing, you understand nothing of the world and you don't have a rock that your fathers take you to. Samira rises to her feet, spits, wipes her mouth with the back of her hand, leaves the boys and girls sitting in the meadow, stamps off.

I don't like the other children, Samira says to her father, slapping the air with her hand.

Let them be, says her father. What do you need the other children for?

Man che midanam, says Samira, shrugs her shoulders.

You do not need them. You need no one, says the commander.

Samira says nothing.

You have me, says the commander. And today I am giving you a new friend.

Who's my old friend? asks Samira.

The commander laughs. Today I am giving you your first friend. The brown horse is going to have its child.

Samira runs into the tent, throws herself into her mother's arms, says, guess what day it is.

I don't know, says Daria, falls silent, goes on whipping the milk in the sheepskin vessel.

You should ask for what reason today is a special day, Samira cries.

For what reason is today a special day? asks Daria, stops whipping the milk, hugs her daughter.

My little horse is going to be born. Samira thinks for a moment and asks, when will it come?

I do not know, says Daria.

Why don't you know? asks Samira.

About birth and death only God knows, says Daria.

That is not true, says Samira. My father knows.

Your father knows everything, says Daria to the simmering water in the pot. The commander knows everything.

When is my horse coming? Samira asks her father.

It will take some time, says her father. Perhaps today, perhaps tomorrow. Samira runs back into the tent to her mother, twists and turns her hand as her father did, says, perhaps it will come today, perhaps it will come tomorrow.

Fine, says Daria, then you do know when your horse is coming.

Sahihst, says Samira, nods.

Daria stirs the rice that she has put in the simmering water. Stirs and stirs so that it does not stick to the bottom of the pot.

Samira stands there and thinks. When is perhaps today, perhaps tomorrow? Samira stands there, brow furrowed, does not know whether she knows now or whether she does not. Then we will just have to be patient and wait, says Samira.

My clever child, says her mother, smiles and spreads her arms, says, come here. Give your mother a kiss and make her happy.

Samira throws herself into her mother's arms, she loves it when her mother wants her to make her happy,

Before her mother can give her a kiss, Samira says, then I am going to the stream now. She leaps to her feet and says, as she runs out of the tent, I'm going to tell the other children we will have to be patient until my horse comes.

A bubble jumps from the simmering, scolding water, throws itself into the fire and dies with a hiss.

We must be patient, Samira calls to the other children. The children are all sitting in a row by the shore. They pay no attention to her.

What are you doing? asks Samira.

We are peeing, says one of the boys.

Samira pulls down her *shalvar*, squats by the water with the other children and pees. One of the boys finishes peeing first, stands up and says, winner. I'm the winner.

Samira looks at the boy, and is about to start scolding and bickering about the fact that they had not even made a bet. Samira opens her mouth, the words stay there. Samira says nothing. She says nothing because she has discovered something that she had not seen properly before. That something dangles between the boy's legs, it is elongated in shape, there is a drop of water hanging from it, the boy takes the thing in his hand, pulls it as though he wanted to tear it off, does not tear it off, lets go of it again, scratches his bum instead. The bum-scratching gives Samira time to take a closer look at the thing. It dangles between the boy's legs, looks like a finger.

What do you need that for? asks Samira. Uncertain whether she wants to hear the answer. Certain that she will not like the answer.

What? asks the boy.

That thing there, says Samira, pointing to the finger between the boy's legs, then finishes peeing, pulls her trousers up so quickly that the boy cannot see that she has no finger hanging beneath her belly.

Haven't you got one? asks the boy. All real boys have one.

Samira does not know what to say. She shrugs her

shoulders, says *diwaneh*, leaves the boy she has called a madman with his finger between his legs and runs back to her tent.

Daria knew the time would come when her daughter would learn that she is different from the other boys. She will stand before her and ask questions. Time and again Daria has wondered what she is to say to her daughter-son when that day comes. Time and again she has found no answer, has thought, I will find an answer when the time comes. Daria has thought her father should explain.

Her little girl stands in front of her with her eyes full of tears and her little shoulders hunched. Daria knows she has heaped guilt upon herself. The mother's heart turns to paper and tears.

The colour has drained from Samira's face. It is as white as the snow that lies in the mountains in winter. Samira swallows down tears. As brave as a big child. As brave as a real boy. Samira does not say much. Asks only, am I not a real boy?

Daria has fear in her eyes.

The child looks at its mother. Full of expectation, full of hope. Hope that its mother will say everything is fine.

Daria looks in her head for words. Words that do not come. However much she searches in her head.

Little Samira stands there, gets smaller and smaller.

Daria wants to go to her child, wants to take it in her arms. Her limbs do not belong to her. Daria stands there, stiff and helpless. Not like an adult. Not like a mother. Not like someone who is supposed to be strong and powerful. Not like someone with answers, someone who is supposed to give protection to her child.

Samira sees everything, needs an answer, needs her

mother, needs that protection. A tear falls from Samira's eye, rolls down her face, falls on the mud floor and disappears. Samira draws all the air she can find around her into her little body, chokes, cries, coughs, wants to suffocate, wants to disappear. Like her tear.

My mother was a stone, Samira will think later.

Samira bends double, the taste of blood comes to her mouth, and finally she cries. The tears are good, they give her strength.

Just enough for a small, big question. Am I not a real boy?

Daria says a lot of little words that no one can hear. Neither herself, nor her daughter. Only one word comes out of her mouth. Only one little word.

Yes.

A small, little Yes. That is all her mother has to say.

Samira trembles, does not know that her body is cold, knows only that her thousand and one questions have no answer.

Daria and Samira stand and stand. Daria does not light the fire, does not knead the dough for the bread, does not spread out the pillows and blankets for the night, does not lower the felt to close up the tent for the night. Samira stands there, trembles, quivers as though winter had entered the tent. Her black eyes plead, and fasten themselves to her stone mother.

Daria knows it is guilt that turns her to stone. Black, heavy guilt. So much guilt that Daria does not see that the commander is standing behind his boy-girl.

Come, boy, says the commander, in a voice that is full of fear. Her father is standing half inside the tent and half outside. The cold in the tent is a wall. His daughter-son stands four paces away from him. The transparent wall of cold keeps him away. Come, boy, he says. Your horse is here.

The father's words touch the child's back. Slowly, so slowly that he himself does not notice, they penetrate the heart of his girl-son, they see the pain, the fear, the sadness, and eat them up. The father's words are an animal, a hungry animal. An animal that devours everything that lives in the heart of the child.

Samira hears it clearly. Her father says, boy.

Slowly, so slowly that she herself does not notice, the tears dry in Samira's dark eyes, which look as though someone had just washed them. She sniffs back the tears in her nose, swallows the rest down. Samira does not know what has happened. She does not know why she has not been able to move. She does not know why now she is able to move again. Slowly, so slowly that she herself does not notice, she moves her fingers, her hand, her arm, she wipes the tears from her face, pulls up her *shalvar* without knowing when and why it has slipped down. Samira opens her mouth, wants to say something, finds the words in her head. She wants to say, I am a real boy. I heard it, my father said it. He said boy.

Samira moves her tongue, opens and closes her mouth. The words do not come out. Samira cannot hear the words that she speaks. Samira says nothing. Remains mute.

Mute. Mute.

A LIE

Samira the mute stretches blades of grass between her thumbs and the balls of her hands, presses her lip against them, blows, plays a tune.

The child is not happy, says Daria.

Leave him alone, says the commander, saddles his horse, calls his girl-son, says, come, boy.

Samira smiles. Boy. That is a beautiful word.

Kommandan koja miri? Commander, where are you riding to? call the people.

Miram sareh kouh. To the mountain, answers the commander. My son and I are riding to our rock.

The father and the son leave the tents, the other *kuchi*, their animals and everything else behind them, they shove their heels into the flanks of the horses, whistle through their teeth, click their tongues and charge off so fast that they fly. Samira knows it, she sees it, they are flying. The hooves of the horses do not touch the ground, the wind blows through their hair, under their shirts, tickles their skin.

The commander bends forward, grips the reins of his

child's horse, urges his stallion on even harder, grips the body of his daughter-son, lifts him into the air, sits him in front of him on his own stallion, holds him tight in his strong arms. Samira closes her eyes, leans back, spreads her arms out, knows it is the truth, it is a lie. A beautiful lie. Flying is when you are high up in the sky. Flying is when you have wings. Angels fly. Samira is not flying. Yet she is. To the very end, to the rock.

Samira does as her father does, she does not put her foot in the stirrup to dismount, swings her leg over the head of the horse and jumps into her father's arms. He grabs his child like a sack of onions and pushes him up on to the flat surface.

Our rock, thinks Samira. It is and it is not. It is, because in all the summers and winters that have come and gone, my father, his father and all our fathers' fathers have come here and it belongs to us.

But the commander also said that all its owners had been firstborn men. Real men. Real men and real sons with their manhood between their legs. Samira has no manhood hanging beneath her belly. Her father has no son. But Samira also knows she is more of a man than many a man with a manhood between his legs. Samira closes her eyes. At what point does a boy become a man?

The commander heaves his powerful body on to the rock, strokes his Samir's head, sees that he has already disappeared into his own world again. I am worried that you will be lost, says the commander, swallows down his tears so that his child does not see them.

A real man does not cry, thinks Samira.

The father kneels in front of his daughter-son, grips him by the arms.

How do I know when his grip is filled with love and when it is not? thinks Samira.

Where are you? asks the commander.

Samira looks at her father, smiles. The most beautiful child's smile in the world. I am in your hands, she thinks.

The commander tightens his grip, shakes his child. Where are you?

Samira sees mountains, valleys, places she has never been, sees people she does not know. I am here and I am not here. What difference does it make where I am? Samira strokes her father's face, touches his long, black curls. I am in the Nowhere, thinks Samira the mute.

Samira the mute does not say a word. She does not say a word because a lifetime is not enough for all the words she would have to say if she could speak. She does not say a word because she does not know where the beginning and the end of her words are. She does not say a word because her father blames her mother. For everything and everyone. Samira does not say a word because it is not her mother's fault. Because it is her fault. Because it is her mother's fault, her father's fault, the world's.

Fault for what?

Fault for everything, for nothing, for whatever.

Why does God send all the questions into my head? thinks Samira. Each of his questions has a thousand and one answers. What is the point of my giving an answer? One and only one of the thousand and one answers that I have.

Her mother had only a small, big Yes.

Daria says, my child does not speak because the injustice we are doing her is so big.

People say, God took away the tongue of the commander's son to test him. God wants to know if he will be enough of a man to be a good commander like his father, although he cannot speak.

Samira does not speak because she does not see the point of saying false words when she knows the truth. Truth is not truth and a lie is not a lie. What is the point of Samira speaking when the people think it is Samir who speaks? If she does not even know herself whether it is Samira who speaks or Samir.

The people ask, Samir, boy, how are you?

Samira smiles and nods. She even nods when she is not feeling good.

That is what people want. So she nods. He is fine, they say.

What are you feeling? asks her father.

Samira smiles.

Is it nice what you are feeling? asks her father. Quietly. Not because it is important. Quietly because the sadness leaves no room in his throat for loud words.

Samira smiles and nods.

All I want is your happiness, says her father.

Happiness, thinks Samira. That is a good word.

I know what makes you happy, says her father, swinging down from the rock. He spreads his arms, says, jump.

Samira stands at the edge of the rock, shuts her eyes, spreads her arms, hears the air move past her and stay with her at the same time, enjoys the moment. Slowly. So slowly that she herself barely notices, Samira lets herself drop forward into her father's strong arms. Happiness is an important word, she thinks, and knows the day will come when she will be too big and her strong father will not be strong enough to catch her.

Her father grabs her, lifts her on to the back of her horse, swings on to his stallion, shoves his heels into its sides, climbs back down the stony piece of mountain on it, as far as the meadow, whistles through his teeth, gallops off, pulls his stallion round, looks at his daughter-son. Samira clicks her tongue, does not shove her heels into her horse's side, pats its neck, climbs down the steep slope on it. Not as quickly, not as surely as her father. The horse slips, stumbles.

Do not be afraid, calls her father.

Samira knows the day will come when she will guide her horse down the rocks just as smoothly and surely, with just as much strength and grace, as her father does.

The commander whistles through his teeth, gallops out into the plain. Urge your horse onwards. Show him who is master, calls the commander. Show him which of you is the stronger.

Samira bends forwards, claws her fingers into her horse's mane, scratches it between the ears, whispers its name. The only word she speaks. Azad.

Azad hears his name, throws his head back, dashes off. Samira slackens the reins so that Azad can stretch its neck as far as it will go.

No boy rides like my Samir, thinks the commander. Smoothly and impetuously. Nimbly, powerfully. United, as one with the animal. Half human, half animal.

Samira sees her father's pride. That is happiness, she thinks. Her heart beats along with the hooves that Azad stamps on the ground, its skin grows hot, becomes damp, its muscles become warm and supple. That is strength, thinks Samira. Strength and power. My Azad and I are preparing ourselves for the game of all games, the game of *buzkashi*. We are preparing ourselves for life. Samira forgets that she is mute. Forgets her thousand and one questions. Forgets that she has no answers. Forgets that she is neither a real boy nor a real girl, forgets her father, her mother sitting in the tent, forgets the guilt. The guilt of everyone and everything.

Samira becomes light. Flies, dissolves into the void. Is everything.

Boy. Come here, boy, calls her father.

Samira does not hear him.

The commander tugs on the reins of his stallion, so that it rises up on its back legs and whinnies. He pulls the animal furiously round, strikes his whip against its neck, dashes off, catches up with his Samir, rides beside him, grabs the reins of Samira's horse, slows both animals until they are almost standing. Samir. Boy. Look at me. Where are you?

That is a big question, thinks Samira, strokes her Azad's mane, presses her head to his neck.

Boy, says the father. Quietly. Because what he has to say is important. You frighten me.

Samira shakes her head.

Her father strokes his girl-boy's damp brow. Let us play *buzkashi*, he says, and does to his daughter-son what his father did to him. He sits on a stone and explains the game. Men play the game to test their mettle, to make themselves stronger. *Buzkashi* is the game with which warriors prepare for the enemy.

Samira narrows her eyes to slits. What battle? What enemy? Is it God's will that the others should be the bad ones and we the good?

You fight over the carcass of a calf or a sheep, says the

commander, your victory is celebrated and you are paid well. A good player is a man blessed with honour and power. Honour, says the commander.

Samira straightens up.

Honour comes to the man who manages to grab the dead animal, which is in the *helal* circle, ride around the post with the scrap of fabric and bring it back to the *helal* circle.

Honour is courage, thinks Samira. Honour is recklessness, honour is both and so much more besides. Honour is everything. Honour is nothing. A big, loud nothing.

Do you know what honour is? asks the commander.

Samira nods.

Honour is when a man achieves his goal. When a man is respected by other men, says the commander.

My father is respected, thinks Samira, because he rides with a carcass to a rag and brings the dead animal to the *helal* circle.

Honour is when a man is full of power and strength, like me, says the commander, clenches his hands into fists, tenses the muscles of his arms, and holds them bent until Samira touches them and nods.

What does God build my father's muscles from? Flesh, bone, skin? Something I do not know? thinks Samira, adds this question to all the other questions in her head. Why do some men have strength in their arms when others do not? Why are there women who are stronger than many men? Yet more questions.

You will see, says the commander, the day will come when you are as strong as I am.

Why is his strength not enough to take the guilt away from my mother? thinks Samira. And why does my mother keep blaming herself rather than passing it on to him, the strong one?

When a man has mastered the game, says the commander, he will also master the enemy.

Samira's eyes are glittering jewels. My father has mastered the game and the enemy, she thinks, wondering why he has not mastered life as well, and does not know how she knows that he has not mastered life.

The commander draws a little circle in the sand with his finger. That is the *helal* circle. At the beginning of the game the dead animal is here. It is been left in the stream all night to wash away the blood, so that its hide is drenched with water, making it even heavier. The commander says nothing more, sees that his Samir is not listening. You are like the water in your mother's pot, he says. You sit there silent and motionless, and yet you are bubbling and seething. I could stop speaking, I could fall silent, and you would not notice. I could go, and you would not miss me.

You are like the bird in the sky. The commander knows only one way to bring the bird down from the sky. He would have to put his rifle to his shoulder, aim at the bird and pull the trigger. With a bullet and a dull, dry bang, he would be able to bring it down to the ground, bring it down to him.

The commander grips his daughter-son by the arms and shakes him. Half with love and longing, half with fury and revulsion.

Samira closes her eyes.

The commander lets go of his child. As soon as the game begins, look neither to left nor to right. Pay no attention to what the other men are doing. Ride off. Men will shout, will try to pull the animal from you. The horses will whinny and snort, will rear up on their back legs, open their eyes and muzzles and look like monsters.

Samira closes her eyes, does not see the monsters, sees the angels that carry her, feels the wind. Samira is above the clouds, near the sun, the moon, the stars. Samira is not afraid, the angels are with her.

Bend low down, says the commander, so that you can grab it securely. Grab the carcass by the leg, pull the animal on to the saddle and wedge it beneath your thighs so that your hands are free to hold the reins and you can wield your whip.

Samira spreads her arms, grabs the hands of the angels who carry her, rises up with them, to the place where there is nothing, the place where the end is. The end of everything and nothing. The end and the beginning. Where God is. Where also God no longer is.

The commander lowers his voice, narrows his eyes to slits as though he is about to reveal a secret. You must get out of the tangle of horses and men as quickly as you can.

Samira straightens up, everywhere there are men on horses, everywhere there are short whips, everywhere there are the faces of monsters.

The commander slashes the air with his whip, says, you give your horse the spur and the whip, trust him, he knows the point you must ride around on the beast. You have shown him the post before, you have ridden again and again around the scrap of cloth with him, he knows the way in his sleep.

Samira, an angel holding each hand, reaches the post with the scrap of cloth, flies back to the circle that is *helal*. Unlike the others who throw the carcass, Samira bends down and lowers it to the ground. Full of respect for the dead animal.

If mute Samira could speak, she would say, respect is when I do not have to put the knife to the animal's throat and slit it open just so that I can play.

Samira was half the size she is now when the commander held her hand in his big, strong man's hand. Very firmly, so that the child could not pull it away. Samira felt the knife force its way through the fur, the skin, the flesh, the throat of the soft lamb.

Samira did it and did not know why. She did it because her father wanted her to.

The commander sat little Samira on her horse and pulled her behind him. Carefully, clumsily. First the lamb fell on the ground, then Samira did. Her father grabbed her and put her back on the horse. Again and again. The sun had gone down long ago, the moon and the first stars were already in the sky when the commander finally sat his daughter-son on his own horse and rode with him through the night.

Daria was standing by the tent. Worried and filled with longing, she spread her arms out wide.

He is asleep, the commander said.

Daria took her daughter-son and said, *koshtish*. You have killed him.

He is asleep, the commander said.

One day you will bring me my child, and it will be dead, Daria said.

The commander wanted to fly into a fury, wanted to put his Daria right, tell her that a woman has no business speaking to her husband like that. Instead he heard his mouth saying words he did not know he had in his head. It will not be your child, I am the one they'll bring home dead to you.

Many summers and winters have come and gone since he said those words. Women, men and children have been brought dead to their mothers, wives, sisters, fathers, brothers and sons. But the commander is just as much alive as he was the evening he said, I am the one they'll bring home dead to you. A cold shiver runs down Daria's beautiful back when she remembers the commander's words.

Daria says, it is not good that you did not keep your words to yourself. When people see things in their heads, find words for them, lay them on their tongues and free them from their mouths, they come true. That is not good. So much is not good.

The days of being laid sleeping in her mother's arms have passed long ago. Samira is no longer a little child. She is taller than her mother, cleverer than her father, stronger than the other boys. Samira is taller and braver than boys who have spent just as many summers and winters on God's earth as she has. She rides faster than many of the other boys, faster than many men. Samira is half man, half woman, with a beauty that enchants both men and women. People call him Samir the beautiful mute.

The women speak behind their hands, say Samir does not need a whip, he does not need to resort to force to control his horse. The men say horses obey him as though he were one of their own, as though he were their leader.

Samira plays a tune on the grass-stalk. The horse talks to Samira the mute. It paws the ground, rears up on its back legs, comes over to her until she feels its breath, until she touches its soft nostrils, hugs its head, strokes its nose. Samira walks along beside the horse, presses her face to its head. The horse looks at her, nibbles at her fingers.

If only I were the horse, the girls say. They say it quietly, so that their fathers and brothers, mothers and sisters do not hear. The women giggle, say, the boy is playing with the horse like a boy in love. The women see the beautiful boy closing his eyes, his breath calming, the world around him falling away. Nothing exists now but the boy and the horse.

The young girls forget to close their mouths, the men see their daughters' longing, their desire, they hiss like snakes, slap them on the back of the head with the palm of their hands. The boy is a devil, the men say. Quietly. So that the commander does not hear.

Daria sees and hears all of that and much else besides.

The boys put their hands on Samira's shoulder. Samira sees the glances of her mother and her father, twists away, shakes off the boys' hands.

It is forbidden for boys to touch girls. The girls' honour is at stake. Touching Samir the boy would be permitted. Samira the mute stares at the ground, bites her lip.

Daria knows the day will come when the boys will be real men and they will not take their hands away from her daughter's shoulder.

People can tell Samir has a secret, and say God has taken away the boy's speech so that he will not reveal his secret to anyone.

The more people speak about a man, the commander says, the more important he is.

Your son is not a man, says Daria.

He will be, says the commander, looking over to his daughter-son, who is sitting in the meadow and playing a tune on a grass-stalk.

Samira does not hear her mother's and her father's words, sees their faces, knows they are ugly words.

Look what you have done, says the commander. You have made him sad again.

Daria says nothing.

Samira knows that her father is blaming her mother. Blaming her for the tune. Blaming her for everything that is yet to come.

Daria leaves the commander standing where he is, goes into the tent to her fire and her water.

The commander does not see her tears, but knows that Daria has tears. She always has tears. Since the day her child stood before her in the tent and she had no answer for Samira. They crouch in her throat, ready to leap out at any moment.

Boy. Stop that, calls the commander. He does not like it when his Samir plays the tune that frees the tears from Daria's throat and brings them to her eyes.

Samira stops. Stops playing.

Azad stops grazing, comes over to her, falls on his knees, lies down on the ground, lays his head in Samira's lap.

Stop that, calls the commander. A horse is a horse. He should carry a man across the plain on his back, he should fight in the game.

Samira does not see her father's fury, does not hear his words.

The commander slashes the air with his whip. What is up with you? he calls. Have you gone deaf as well?

Daria comes out of the tent. Leave him alone, she says.

Leave me alone, says the commander.

Daria leaves him alone and says nothing.

Samira pushes Azad out of her lap, rises to her feet as he does, forces herself on to his unsaddled back, clicks her tongue, rides away.

The commander slashes the air with his whip, whistles for his stallion, forgets that he has tied it to the stake. The horse pulls on its rope and opens its eyes wide. The commander hurries to untether it, leaps on to its back, follows his girl-boy. Daria sits in her tent, by the fire and her pot with the simmering water, looks outside, sees her child, sees her commander, does not catch the bubble that jumps from the fire.

The commander catches up with his daughter-son, rides beside him, grabs his Samir, sits him in front of him on the back of his stallion and holds him tightly. Very tightly, so that he does not fall off. So that he does not jump off.

Let us ride to our rock, says Samira's father, presses his arm so tightly around Samira that she can hardly breathe.

Samira claws her fingers into the mane of her father's stallion, presses her face to the animal's hide, strokes it, sees her Azad alongside her. Azad has stopped galloping and is growing slower. The more Samira strokes her father's stallion, the slower Azad becomes, and the slower her father's stallion becomes as well. The commander strikes his whip against his stallion's thigh, pulls and tugs at the reins. The stallion refuses to obey, slows down. Samira straightens up, swings her leg over the stallion's head, jumps off. The commander pulls hard on the reins, comes to a standstill, jumps off as well.

Samira stands there with her Azad behind her. The horse pushes its head over her shoulder, she puts her arm around it. Her father's stallion pushes his nose into Samira's hand, nibbles at her fingers.

Animals understand you, says the commander, and does not know where all his hatred is coming from. It is hatred, bigger and stronger than himself, that he carries within him for the enemy. It is hatred that frightens him.

The horses scrape the ground with their hooves, take a step backwards. Samira stands like a tree.

Stop that, says her father. The commander is not asking Samira. It is an order.

What is she supposed to stop? Being a tree? Being Samira? Being Samir? Being a real boy? Being alive? What?

Stop that, says her father.

Samira the mute lowers her eyes.

Horses are horses, says the commander.

Samira the mute raises her eyes, narrows them to slits, does only that.

The commander slashes the air with his whip. Stop that, he says, in a voice so loud and ugly that the taste of blood comes to his throat.

The commander draws back his arm, goes to strike the stallion with his whip. Samira's eye follows her father's whipping arm. The commander raises his arm high and higher, into the sky so that God can see his whip. The commander is about to let out all his rage, he is about to strike, when the stallion opens its eyes wide, rears up on its hind legs, whinnies, dashes off.

The commander's whipping arm stays in the air.

It is God that holds his hand, thinks Samira.

A PREMONITION

To ensure that death is quick, Samira sharpens the already sharpened knife, gives one last, merciful sip of water to the animal, which after all has also been created by God, grips it by the legs, jerks them out from under its body so that it falls on to the ground, presses her knee to its chest, puts the knife to its neck, whispers a mute *be-isme-Allah*, and with one quick cut slits the sheep's throat. It wriggles and groans, blood bursts from its neck, runs over Samira's hand, on to the ground in front of her feet. The animal waves its legs around in the air, opens its eyes, sees its murderer.

That is the way of life, thinks Samira the mute. Life is killing, life is being killed.

God bless the sacrificial blood, says her father.

Samira catches the first of the blood in the bowl, gives it to the circle, which is *helal*, the rest she tips in front of her tent, so that everyone can see it is a warrior's tent. Samira leads her own horse and her father's horse across the blood, walks across it herself. Four times, so that God will forgive her. For the sacrificial blood she has spilt. Blood as red as the blood that flows in her own veins.

Stop that, says the commander. That is enough respect.
Samira stops.

Come on, says the commander. The other boys are waiting.

He stands beside the playing-field and looks at his Samir. My son is invincible, he says to himself.

Samira bends low over her horse's neck, does not tug at the reins, does not shove her heels into his sides, does not beat his sides with the short *buzkashi* whip. It looks as though Samira gallops in a straight line. In fact she sways from side to side, drives away the other boys as though this were a dance she was performing, not a battle that she had to win.

Look at him, says the commander, my son is lithe as a fish in water, light as a bird in the air.

The other men nod.

Olfat the ugly turns away so that the commander cannot hear him, says, the day will come when his son will have to ride in the real game, when a hundred and more riders fight him for the carcass. That is the day when he will lose.

The other men say nothing, they are afraid, they do not want Samir to lose. He will be their new leader when the commander no longer leads them, because if Samir does not do it, Olfat will do it. Olfat and his four sons. Olfat the liar, the dishonoured. Olfat the thief.

The men want to believe in the power, the invincibility of the commander's son. They want Samir to take the place of his father, to protect their families, their property and possessions, from the enemy and from Olfat and his four sons. Look at him, say the men, he is still a boy, he is a long way from being a real man, but by God, his body is already full of power, his spirit is full of confidence and his heart is full of goodness.

Olfat spits, greenish-yellow, it lies at his feet. Look at him, he says with a stinking laugh. See the way he treats horses. Gently, soft-heartedly. The boy is not a real lad. And he will never be a real man.

The men turn away, do not want to see the greenish-yellow from Olfat's throat, do not want to smell his breath, say, Samir is just, he is decent. They say it quietly, so that Olfat does not hear, but say it loudly enough, so that the commander hears it.

Olfat pushes his way back into the circle of men, forces them to listen to him, says, our commander is not a real man himself. He has only fathered a single son, and he has lost his manhood as well.

Samira does not hear the words, but knows about them. The good ones and the bad ones. She knows that Olfat's words are ugly. As ugly as the greenish-yellow that he spits, that lies on the meadow like an ugly frog with its skin torn open, a frog that wants to die.

Samira the mute likes being mute because she has no answer either to the words that are ugly, nor to the words that are not. If it is up to her, she will not be anything at all. Neither a good nor a bad leader, neither a good nor a bad warrior. She has enough responsibility already, Samira thinks. People should be satisfied with all the trouble she takes to be as everyone wants her to be.

Samira looks across towards ugly Olfat, urges her horse onwards so that it rides even faster. Her father sees it, the men see it, Olfat the ugly sees it too. The commander is pleased, the men are pleased. Only ugly Olfat is not pleased.

Daria sits in her tent by the fire, does not catch the bubble that jumps from the pot, lets it jump into the fire to die with a hiss. Daria does not see ugly Olfat's face, she does not see the greenish-yellow, but she knows it is there. Daria does not hear what the men are saying, but knows it is there, knows it is not good for her child.

The commander says, my Samir is a winner.

Daria hears her commander's words, hears the battering hooves of the horse, hears her child's breath. She wants to go to the child, wants to say, stop it, you will kill yourself. Does not do it, watches the bubbles instead. Daria lets her child fight. Lets the bubbles jump. Lets her commander hope. Lets the men talk. Lets Olfat spit. Daria lets everything happen. Daria heaps guilt upon herself.

Who won? asks Daria, when Samira and the commander come back to her in the tent.

Samira smiles.

The commander says nothing, acts as though he had not heard his wife's question.

So my child won, says Daria. The child's victory is the joy in the mother's life.

Samira smiles, hugs her mother, full of forgiveness. Forgiveness for the blame the father heaps on his Daria. Samira loves the game of forgiveness. Loves being a child. Samira sees the father, sees his expression, full of jealousy, full of self-doubt.

Leave her in peace, says Daria.

The commander does not hear his wife's words. Does not want to hear them.

You have our child all day, says Daria. You tug at her, chase her up and down hill on the horse. All day she is supposed to be a man. Shoot. Hunt. Kill. Play men's games.

Leave her alone. Just for a little bit of the day, let her be my girl too.

The commander does not hear.

Daria sits by her fire, lets the bubbles jump, lets them die.

Boy, look at me, says the commander. He is not asking his son. It is an order.

Samira obeys.

Go and sleep, says her father. Before dawn we will ride into the mountains, to our rock.

Samira obeys, wants to spread out her blankets for the night.

Stop that, says the commander. He is not asking. It is an order.

Samira stops.

Spreading out the bedding is women's work, says the commander.

Daria rises to her feet. With difficulty, she props her hand on her knee, sighs, wipes her forehead with the back of her hand. Daria bears a burden on her shoulders that is as heavy as the rocks in the mountains.

Samira does not know when it happened, when her mother became an old woman, when she lost her strength. Samira wants to push her back to her place by the fire, wants her mother from Before, wants to disappear into the world of sleep in her mother's arms. She wants to stand up to her father, tell him to leave her mother alone. Does not do it, just stands there, in the very place where she stood when she was less than half as tall as she is today and does not know the day when everything was lost.

The commander is just dipping his warm bread, which Daria has pulled from the oven-hole in the floor, into the fresh yoghurt that she has been beating all day from goat's milk. He is about to put the yoghurt-soaked bread in his mouth. Daria has just spread the blankets for her child out on the floor. Daria is just casting a tired glance at the commander, when Samira grabs her rifle, puts it over her shoulder, walks purposefully out of the tent, neither quickly nor slowly, whistles to her horse, swings on to its back, rides off into the dark of night.

The commander commits a sin, throws his bread into the fire, into his Daria's fire, rises up. Wants to leave the tent, wants to ride after his Samir, when he feels his wife's hand on his arm.

You see? says the commander. You see what you've done to my son?

Daria wants to say how great her pain is, when her eyes catch the commander's eyes and she sees the grief in them. The grief and the longing. Why is Before always better than Now? she asks.

The commander does not understand.

Daria does not know where the words in her head come from, does not know the reason why her tongue utters them. They are words she uttered back then. Words she had forgotten long ago. I miss you, she says.

The commander says nothing, swallows down tears. I'm here, can you not see me? he says, amazed that his voice has lost its fury.

Yes I can. That's all that Daria says. Just a small and insignificant Yes I can.

Up on the rock Samira thinks, spreading my blankets is my business. She cocks her rifle, lays it beside her, looks into the sky, talks to God and the stars.

Back in the tent Daria says, the child is not a child any more.

I know, says the commander.

Daria does something that she has not done in a long time, pulls her dress over her head, is half naked.

The commander puts his fingers to his Daria's skin, lets them do what they want. Daria says nothing, her hand wanders down the commander's neck, across his chest, wanders lower down to where the shot landed in the commander's body. Where there is nothing now. Just scars, craters and wounds.

The commander twitches, says, you have lost your longing for me.

It is there, you just do not see it, says Daria.

It is not my fault, says the commander.

Daria knows who is at fault. It is shame, hatred. The commander hates the man who fired, his men who laid him in front of the tent rather than let him die. He hates Bibi-jan for giving Daria the amulet, he hates his wife for heaping guilt upon him. He hates the people who do not see him as a real man. The commander hates his Samir for not being a real boy. The commander hates everything and everyone, hates himself and every-thing that has happened, hates everything that has not happened.

The commander has become one with the Nothing where once his manhood was. I have lost the man in me, says the commander.

Daria does not want him to say it. Things come true when you say them. We've lost our child, she says.

I have not lost my son, says the commander.

She does not belong to us, says Daria.

He is my son, says the commander.

Long before the sun comes over the mountain, the commander swings on to his stallion, rides through the dark to his rock. To his Samir.

Samira smiles when she hears the hooves and the snorting of her father's stallion.

The commander stands at the foot of his rock, staring into the dark of night. All of a sudden, not knowing any longer why he has come to his Samir, stretches out his arms, jumps, wants to grab the edge of the rock, slips, jumps again, touches the edge with his fingertips, cannot get hold of it, knows his son has known for a long time that this is the day when little Samir must become a man, because his father has ceased to be one. The commander is neither sad, nor feels pain. He feels light. He whistles for his stallion, swings on to its back, stands upright, pulls himself up on to the rock as he did when he was a little boy.

Wake up, my son, your father is here, whispers the commander. Samira pretends to be asleep, pretends she has not known for a long time that the commander is no longer invincible. Samira turns around, smiles.

You still have your old smile, says the commander. I held you in my arm, you took my thumb in your little hand, smiled, laid your head on one side and went to sleep. When was that? Twelve or perhaps even only eleven summers and winters that have come and gone?

Samira pulls on one of her father's curls, shrugs her shoulders.

You're right, says the commander. What difference does it make? None. None at all.

The commander looks at his Samir, sees the young woman in him, sees the young man in his daughter. Knows he will never be either one or the other. Do you feel it? asks the commander. God has removed the veil that he suspended between you and me.

Samira the mute laughs, puts her hand in front of her eyes, as though her fingers were the veil.

The commander falls silent. Forgive me, he says at the end of his silence.

Samira the mute smiles.

The commander has brought a bundle, gives it to his daughter-son, says the day will come when you will open this bundle. That will be the day when you make a decision.

Samira the mute smiles.

I must go to war, says the commander.

Samira the mute nods.

The war is a place from which one may not come back.

Samira nods, pretends to fire a gun, pretends to be hit, collapses.

Does that not frighten you?

Samira the mute shakes her head.

I could be killed.

Samira shakes her head, touches her father's powerful muscles.

Let us call the sun, says her father, spreading his arms wide. Like before. Like before, he wants to take his child in his arms, close his eyes, ask, what do you feel?

Samira does not throw herself into her father's arms, she does not let him hug her, she jumps from the rock, disappears into the darkness.

The sun's first light is just lifting the darkness from the black sky and tinting it blue, the silhouette of the mountain is just standing out against the first light, when he sees his Samir climbing nimbly and deftly like a goat up to the peak.

At the very top Samira comes to a stop. Silent, immobile, upright like a narrow rock, she stands there with her back to her father, facing the sun. The sun rises over the mountain, awakens the grass, the undergrowth, the bushes. The world wakes up, warms up, the light becomes harsh, hurts the eyes. Samira turns round, spreads her arms and legs, stands before the sun, casts a long shadow. Pearls of water stand out on the commander's brow, the blood rushes in his veins, his breathing grows heavy, his tongue grows thick, he tries to swallow, cannot. The horses scrape the ground with their hooves, lift and lower their heads so that their manes fly, the shadow grows, lengthens, creeps across the rocks. The sun is a big, gleaming ball. Samira stands in the middle of the bright sphere, stands in the middle of the sun.

My son has become an angel, whispers the commander. He sits in his daughter-son's shadow, stares up to the peak, says, forgive me.

The sun rises, with her arms spread wide Samira stands there as if she is carrying the sun.

You have broken through the light of the sun, then you have carried it, says the father when his Samir swings effortlessly on to the rock. The commander lays his head on the shoulder of his daughter-son, becomes a child. When did that happen? asks the commander. I did not know you don't need to climb on your horse's back to get up on the rock.

Samira the mute shrugs her shoulder.

When did you lose the child in you? asks her father.

Samira jumps down from the rock, does not swing on to the back of her own horse, swings on to the back of her father's stallion, looks up to the rock, bows to her father, the commander, the invincible, rides off.

The commander looks after her until she is only a tiny dot.

Samira pulls the stallion's head round, dashes back to the rock and her father. Beneath the rock the stallion rises up on its back legs, whinnies, waves its front legs in the air as though it wants to jump on to the rock.

Before I go to war I will take part in a game of *buzkashi*, says the commander. It will be my last game. And when I return, you will be the one who is going to play.

Samira the mute smiles, knows she will never be playing as long as the commander is in the game.

Come, says the father. I am tired. Let us go and lie in the sun on the rock and wait for the birds.

Samira the mute obeys. The father and his daughter-son lie on their backs, look into the blue sky, do as the father had said, wait for the birds. Only the wind and their breathing can be heard.

Samira is the first to spot the bird. Very high up, higher than Samira has ever seen one, a huge silver bird is flying without beating its wings. Samira stretches out her arm, follows it with her finger.

That is not a bird, says her father. That is an aeroplane.

Samira the mute frowns.

Poor boy, says the commander. Look what I have done to you. You do not even know what an aeroplane is. But you know what cars are, do you not?

Samira nods. Up in the mountains there are no cars, but when they move to the South of the country in the winter, Samira sees cars. Cars are boxes with thick black wheels underneath. Cars are made of iron, are stronger and faster than the fastest horses. They carry people, their tents and all their belongings from one place to another. Samira likes cars.

You see, says the father. And that thing up there in the sky is a kind of car, only it is much bigger. It has wings and it can fly.

Samira did not know that. She did not know that there were cars that had wings and could fly.

There are not many men who can fly aeroplanes, says the commander. They are called a *pilot*.

Pilot, thinks Samira, that is a beautiful name.

A MIRACLE

The commander has forgotten long ago what war he is fighting. Who he is killing, and who he is killing for. Who he is willing to be killed for himself. Since he was a boy he has been fighting. His father became a Mujahed and went to the mountains, killed Russians. The little commander's son stayed with his mother, protected her and his sisters and brothers. For ten long years Russian soldiers carried off Afghan girls and women, raped them, slit them open.

When the Russians left his country, the young commander's son thanked his God and thought the war had gone with them. He had just taken his weapon from his shoulder. His father had just said, peace is when we build our tents, milk the goats, play *buzkashi*.

The young commander's son had just begun to get answers to his questions when his father said, we must go back into the mountains. This time the young commander's son went with his father, fought other Afghans. A shot was fired, a shot which hit his father. The boy pushes earth over his dead father, asks who are we killing our brothers for, when the other men say, we must fight the Taliban.

The commander just says, I am not fighting any more. I am not killing a brother any more when the other men say, we are fighting foreigners. We are fighting foreign Talib. The commander just says, I am not killing any Moslems, while God sends drought and hunger and kills the seeds in the fields. The other men say, we must fight to survive.

And now? Now he is still fighting. Against whoever. What counts is that he is fighting. Not for the freedom of his homeland and the true Islam. The commander is fighting only for money and nothing else. For little money. Money that is not even enough to buy the loyalty of his men.

This time it is a good war, says the commander, running his hand over Samir's close-cropped head.

I did not know that war could be good, says Daria.

The other men say the foreigners are paying for this war, says the commander.

I thought we did not want any foreigners in our homeland, says Daria.

They want to free our country, says the commander.

Who do they want to free us from? asks Daria.

The commander shrugs.

Daria says nothing.

Samira jumps up, grabs her rifle and the belt with the remaining four cartridges, stands in front of her father.

No, says her father. You are not coming.

Would she speak, Samira would say, I want to kill so that you may live. Samira the mute stays mute.

The night has not yet gone, the stars still hang in the black sky, when outside the tent there is the clatter of horses' hooves and the quiet chatter of men. They are the commander's men, Raouf the clever, Habib the kind, Olfat the ugly with his four sons. They are loyal and disloyal men. They are men who want the commander to lead them. They are men who want to lead themselves.

The commander greets each of them with a smile and a hug, he also hugs Olfat the ugly and his four sons.

We are ready, says Habib the kind.

Have some tea, says the commander.

Komandan, what do you think? Will we be well paid? asks the first son of Olfat the ugly.

The commander knows the question is a trap.

The other men say nothing. It is not the business for sons to speak in the presence of older and important men. It is not the business for sons to put questions to the commander.

Komandan, the first son of Olfat the ugly says again. You are our leader. You are responsible for us. Will we be well paid?

The commander narrows his eyes to slits, says, *bache*. He says nothing more. Says only, boy. It is like a shot. A small and well-aimed shot.

The first son of Olfat the ugly twitches, lowers his eyes.

The commander leans forward, says, look at me. It is an order that he is issuing to the son of Olfat the ugly.

The first son of Olfat the ugly raises his eyes.

The commander straightens up, asks, have you been paid up to this day?

The first son of Olfat the ugly lowers his eyes, says nothing.

Answer, says the commander.

Samira hears the beating of hearts. Her own, that of the first son of Olfat the ugly, her mother's, her father's. The beating of all the other hearts.

The commander waits.

Bale, yes, says the first son of Olfat the ugly. Quietly.

The commander nods. Says nothing.

Samira hears the beating of hearts.

The commander drinks a sip of his tea, looks one after the other into the eyes of each of the men sitting around him, says, I do not know whether people are telling the truth, or whether they are just saying all the things they are saying just to make themselves important. I do not know the foreigners. I do not know why they have come to our homeland. I do not know how much money they have brought with them. The commander holds his empty glass in the air, waits for his Daria to fill it with fresh tea. All I know, says the commander, is I will lead you as I have always led you.

The men say nothing.

God is my witness, says the commander. On my son's life, I will bear responsibility for you as I always have.

Habib the kind nods, sits up, says, you speak well.

The commander says nothing, strokes his beard.

Olfat the ugly narrows his eyes, says, you speak well. You are responsible for us, so tell us what we should do when these foreigners come up to our highlands. Should we hide our women and daughters, our property and our animals?

The commander does something that he has never done before when sitting with his men. He speaks in a voice that is loud and full of rage. In a voice that makes everyone and everything fall silent. The foreigners will not come, says the commander. Yet does not know how he knows they will not come.

Samira hears the beating of hearts.

They will not come, because we will go to them. *Bass* and *khalass*. That is all.

Habib the kind is the first to nod. Raouf the clever nods. All the other men nod. Even Olfat the ugly and his four sons nod.

Who are we going to fight? asks one of the men.

For whoever, and against whoever, says the commander.

When will we fight? asks one of the men.

When the sun comes, says the commander. We will pray and go to war.

In the morning the commander peels himself out of his blankets, puts his rifle over his shoulder, ties up the bundle of the bread that his Daria has pulled out of the oven, climbs on to his horse, rides off. Down into the valley, into the village, to war. The commander is not sitting straight-backed on the stallion, he is not hopeful that he will win, that he will defeat the enemy as he has done before. Whoever the enemy may be.

Everything is as it always is when the commander goes to war. Yet everything is different than it always is. The commander misses his Samir, his upland plain in the mountains of the Hindu Kush, his rock. The commander longs for the man he was Before, many summers and winters ago. He longs for the strength that he had within him Before, the strength he has lost.

Samira and Daria squat in their tent. Daria kneads the dough for the bread, makes little round lumps, presses them flat, slaps them against the wall of the oven. The oven her commander built for her. You will see, time will take wing and fly away, says the mother. You will not even notice that he has gone, and he will be back again.

Samira squats in front of her mother, wraps her arms

around her legs, rests her head on her knees. Daria pulls the baked bread out of the oven, tears off a little piece, hands it to her daughter-son. Samira likes it when the bread is fresh, still warm and soft. Before, when she was half as big as today, before she was mute, she would smile, press the warm bread to her chest, and say, your bread warms my heart. Today Samira is mute, today her heart is cold.

Her mother has spoken the truth. The days and nights take wing, become birds, fly away. The moon becomes thin. Samira sits in the darkness on the rock, hears the hooves of the horses, the hooves of her father's stallion. Samira jumps from the rock, swings on to the back of her horse, rides towards the men. They are riding quickly. Quietly. Not speaking to one another.

The commander does not stop, goes past his son, no greeting, no hug, no stories from the war. Samira urges her horse on. She knew. This time it is different from Before. Samira the mute does not understand, does not swallow down the tears, lets them flow, urges her horse on, rides past her father and his men, dashes to her tent, to her mother.

Daria is standing outside her tent in the darkness.

Samira does not wait for her horse to stop, she jumps from its back, runs past her mother, runs into the tent, past her mother's cold fire. The pot is in its place, the water is in the pot, it does not simmer and scold. Is silent. Is cold. Not one bubble leaps out of the pot to land in the fire and die with a hiss.

Samira's heart is cold. Cold like the fire, cold like the water. Samira stumbles, falls, creeps into the corner between blankets and pillows, makes herself small, shuts her eyes, wants to see nothing, to hear nothing, hears only the cold beating of a heart. Her own heart.

Daria comes into the tent. Her face has lost its colour.

Samira knows her father did not greet her mother either, did not fold her in his arms, has not told her either of the war.

Daria finds her child. Come, she says.

Samira does not move, stays between the blankets.

The mother sits in front of Samira, sees her beautiful face, her soft features that have hardened because she is outside all day, rides wildly, climbs on the mountains, because she shoots, fights with the other boys, because she chops wood, because she has become a boy. Her child's beautiful dark eyes glitter wildly, her little nose has become wide and hard because she has fights with the other boys, her beautiful lips are coarse and torn because she always bites them, because she always has the short whip for the *buzkashi* game or the reins of her horse between her teeth.

Samira sees her mother's expression, knows that God has removed the veil that he had suspended between her and her mother.

Daria rises, draws her child up, goes out of the tent, pulls her child behind her. Stands there. Samira does not know why the men are still sitting on their horses. She leaves her mother standing there, looks for her father. She wants to look into his face, find the reason for his silence. Samira's father's stallion recognises her, calls to her with a quiet whinny. Samira stretches out her hand, touches the cloth which is draped over the back of her father's stallion, touches the blood, feels the body under the cloth, knows it is her father. Her father, the commander, the invincible.

Samira's mouth gapes open wide, wants to scream. No sound comes from her throat. Samira screams mutely. Draws a breath. Opens her mouth again. Again not a sound comes from her throat. The taste of blood comes into her mouth. Samira the mute screams. Samira falls, stays on the ground, creeps like an animal that has been hit by a bullet, creeps over to her mother, lies at her feet, claws the mother-skirt, pulls her mother down to her, stares into her mother's eyes that are filled with grief, opens her mouth, says, blood has been spilt.

A miracle has happened, says one of the men. The mute Samir is speaking.

Your father has become a *shahid*, says Daria. Apart from that she says nothing. Does not ask why her child speaks. For what reason it has not spoken for all the summers and winters that have come and gone. Daria does not say a miracle has happened.

The men lay the commander's corpse on the ground outside the tent, in the exact spot where they laid him once before.

Daria screams, throws herself on the dead commander, pulls at her hair until she holds bunches of it in her hands, claws her fingers in his shroud, tugs at it, pulls it open, claws in his clothes, scratches her own face until it bleeds, until a drop of her blood falls on her commander's face, lies there, mingles with his blood, becomes one.

Samira wants to do as her mother does, like her wants to throw herself on the dead commander, wants to weep, wants to lament, wants to scratch her face till it bleeds. Samira does not do any of that. She just keeps standing. Watches her mother and her dead father. It is as though she were standing down in the valley, in the bazaar, watching the strolling musicians who have come from the big city to tell the mountain people stories from the *Shahnameh*, the letter of the king.

Daria throws herself on the ground, strikes her head against the stone that lies in front of her until the blood from her forehead turns the stone red.

Where is God? asks Samira, puts her girl-boy's hand on her mother's head.

Her mother stares out of crazed eyes, babbles words that Samira does not know, pushes her daughter-son away from herself. Half without intention, half not. Roughly. Samira's heart stays cold.

The men carry their bullet-riddled commander into his tent. Blood drips on to the floor. Commander's blood. Sacrificial blood.

Bibi-jan comes, washes the dead man's ragged face, wraps a white cloth round the head, ties it round his chin so that his dead mouth does not spring open, strokes the commander's head like Before when he was a little boy.

Olfat the ugly says, we need a new leader.

The other men cry, say, it is time for the boy to become a man. A real man. He shall lead us. He is the son of our honoured commander.

Olfat the ugly says, he is still a child.

The more people come to see the dead invincible, the further away Samira moves from her dead father and her mother who is scratching her face open. Samira goes out into the dark of night, fetches the bundle that her father gave her on the rock, goes to the stream. She wants to open the bundle, knows it is not the right day yet, takes off her boy's cap, takes off her shoes, takes off her *shalvar-kamiz*, lies down in the cold water, closes her eyes and does what she has not done for all the summers and winters that have come and gone. She speaks. Samira has not spoken to anyone, now she speaks to the water.

Wash me, she says, wash my sins, take them with you, take the questions that have no answer, take the pain, take the girl in me. Take. Take whatever you want. Give me room. Room for my life without father, room to be able to be a boy. A real boy.

Samira sees her small breasts, knows that the water will not take them away. Samira knows that they are getting bigger, that she must hide them. Samira lies in the water, knows that she should weep, does not know why she is laughing instead. Samira stays in the cold water until her body hurts, until she no longer feels it, until she knows nothing any more, wants to know nothing any more, until she loses all questions, wants no further answers.

The mullah has come to conduct the funeral. He is about to ask for what reason the commander's son is not coming to his father's funeral when a shadow falls upon the cloth in which the dead man lies. The mullah narrows his eyes, sees the outline of a boy who is not yet a man. The sun is a great gleaming ball. Samira is standing in the middle of the bright sphere. It is as though an angel has appeared. It is as though the devil has appeared.

Salam. That is all that Samira says. Just a small, big *salam.* Samira looks at the mullah. The mullah knows she is looking straight through him.

A miracle has happened, say the women and men. The mute Samir is speaking.

Sit down next to me, says the mullah. We want to pray.

Daria is squatting behind the men, next to the women. She has pulled a black cloth over her head, rocks her body back and forth. Samira sees her mother's pain, which is so great that it is nearly killing her. Samira goes over to her mother, grabs her arms with a firm grip. The mother's arms have become thin. It is not your fault, says the daughter, leads the mother to where the men are sitting, to where the mullah sits, to where her dead father lies.

What is the woman doing in our rows? ask the men.

Samira pushes her mother next to the mullah on the floor, squats down next to her. The mullah edges up, wants to say something. His eyes catch the dark eyes of the commander's son. The mullah says nothing.

The men speak quietly so that Olfat the ugly cannot hear them. He will assume his father's legacy and lead us.

The mullah rocks his body back and forth, puts a hand to his ear, wants to begin to pray. Before the first stinking note comes from his throat, another voice rings out. It sounds like the song of God's *houris*, the angels he has sent to sing the life and death of the commander. It is Samira's voice.

Daria's heart becomes a bud, opens up, glows.

Night has fallen long since, the other women and their children, the men and their rifles are in their tents. Daria and Samira sit in front of the heaped-up hill of earth beneath which the dead commander lies. Samira puts wood on the fire, does not look at the hill of earth, does not want to see it, sees only her mother and the fire dancing on her face as though it were at a feast of joy.

Daria moves her lips, babbles words that Samira does not understand, the amulet will protect my child, says her mother, and destroy everything and everyone that wants to do my child harm.

I will protect you, says Samira.

My brave girl, says Daria. She does not say, my brave child. Does not say, my brave boy. Says, my brave girl.

Samira does not think about it, presses up against her mother, puts her head in her lap, shuts her eyes, breathes violently, does not swallow down the tears. Weeps. Weeps until each tear becomes a red flower.

At the end of four days and nights that Daria and Samira spend with the dead man, the mother asks her child, for what reason did you not speak?

Man che midanam, what do I know? says Samira. She shrugs her shoulders. That was how God willed it. She lays her head in her mother's lap.

Your head in my lap is like Before, when you were a little child.

Before no longer exists, says Samira. That is how life goes. Life is killing. Life is being killed.

How do you know that? asks Daria.

Samira sees all the sheep she has killed, lined up in a row. Sees the throats gaping open like laughing red mouths. Smells the blood of the sacrificed.

Man che midanam, she says, closes her eyes, hears a voice. It is the voice of the invisible listener.

You are clever, he says. Cleverer than your poor mother, cleverer than your dead father.

Man che midanam, says Samira.

Daria runs her hand over her girl's head, says, sleep.

Who are you? asks Samira.

You know me, says the voice. I am the invisible listener. How do you know that life is killing, that life is being killed?

I have seen it, says Samira, claws her hand into her mother's skirt.

I know, says Daria, your poor eyes have seen much. Stop fighting. Sleep.

The invisible listener is with me, says Samira.

Send him away, says Daria. Tell him you want to sleep. Tell him to leave you alone.

My mother says I am to send you away, says Samira.

First you were mute, now you are talking in your sleep, says Daria.

He is going to tell me everything, says Samira.

Tell him you do not want to know, says her mother.

The invisible listener squats on the hill of earth beneath which the dead commander lies, plucks a blood-red flower, throws it in Samira's face.

Samira twitches, clutches harder at her mother-skirt.

Look, says the invisible listener. Look and tell me what you see.

I see my father. I see my mother. I see the battle they have fought.

My child has a guest, says Daria. She talks to the fire, because there is no one else there for her to talk to.

Who is the guest? asks the fire.

It is the invisible listener, says Daria.

What does he want from her? asks the fire.

He wants her to see, says Daria.

Poor Daria. You have lost your mind, says the fire.

Daria shrugs her shoulders. I have lost my child. I have lost the angel that lives in me.

The fire crackles, the flames squabble and hiss.

Shsh, quiet. My child is sleeping, says Daria.

The invisible listener is no longer squatting on the hill of earth, he is squatting on the fire, looks at Samira, asks, did you see?

Samira nods. I saw the guilt.

Whose guilt? asks the invisible listener.

The guilt of my mother, the sin and the guilt of my father. The sin and the guilt of God.

The invisible listener squats on Samira's chest.

My poor girl, says Daria.

The invisible listener puts his finger on Samira's mouth. Tell her you are not a poor girl.

A tear jumps from Daria's eye on to her daughter's face. Samira opens her eyes, wipes her mother's tears from her face, says, I did not know that I can cry in my sleep.

The listener comes and stands behind Daria, puts his face on her shoulder.

Samira sees her mother and beside her the face of the invisible listener, stretches out her fingers, wants to touch his face. He disappears, then reappears, lays his face in her mother's lap, very close. Samira feels his breath, hears his heart. The invisible listener speaks in a low voice. Tell your mother it is time to give you the amulet because it destroys and destructs all that wants to harm you.

At the end of four days and four nights Daria and Samira return to their tent. Daria lights her fire, fills her pot with water, puts it on the fire. Samira collects the horses, swings on to the back of her father's stallion, rides, dashes across the plain until she flies.

That's him, say the people, that's the commander's son and his horses.

The people know what needs to be done. For forty days and nights of mourning they leave the widow Daria alone. They do not say, your provider has died, do not ask, what's going to become of you now. They do not say, we cannot even provide for our own families, none of us can protect you. They do not say, you need a new protector.

At the end of forty days and nights they come. The mothers of the unmarried sons, the main wives and the sisters of the other men. You must marry, they say. You need a provider, a protector.

I am not without protection, says Daria. I have a son.

Your son is a child, say the other women. God does not like to see when a woman is alone and without the protection of a man. It brings disorder. Strange men will come, will want you, and there will be war between our men and the others.

The elders, the *rish-sefid*, and the other men gather. Women are forbidden to take part. The wife of the dead commander sits apart from them. It is enough if your son takes part in our *shura*, say the men. He is not a man yet, but now that the mute Samir is speaking again, he should speak.

Olfat the ugly says, the woman and her child shall be under my protection. My first son will take leadership, it is my family's right to take on the commander's horses and property. The man with the whitest beard says, I have been alone for many summers and winters. It will please God if I take them. Another man says, how do you know what God likes and what he does not?

Many men speak many words.

Samira keeps silent.

The men say, speak. Your mother said you would protect her. Now you are not even speaking.

Samira says neither yes nor no, she says, I have heard you. I will make a decision and tell you of it.

The men fall silent. None of them had expected such a big answer.

Olfat the ugly asks, when will you tell us of your decision?

When the right time for a decision has come, says

Samira. In a voice that is clear and distinct. Full of courage. Full of confidence in herself.

When will the right time for a decision have come? asks Olfat the ugly and spits.

Samira does not reply, rises to her feet, bows, asks for permission to leave, does not wait for permission. Goes.

You have courage, says the mother, and leans her tired head against her daughter's shoulder. They will come again, what will you do? Daria does not say, what will we do, she says, what will you do. You. Big and heavy.

The right thing. I will do the right thing, says Samira.

Again the moon is full. Again it is as it has been every night since the commander has been under the earth. Daria lies under her blankets, sleeps, moans and weeps in her sleep. Samira squats next to the entrance, where her father sat, says, God is great, he will help us. I am with you. Sleep. I will protect you. Samira squats and protects her mother until she does not know whether she is asleep or awake, squatting or lying down.

The moon is just disappearing behind a cloud, a little breeze is just blowing, Daria is moaning again, when the horses scrape the ground with their hooves, whinny quietly. Four strange shadows flit around the tent in the darkness. The dead commander's stallion raises and lowers its head so that its mane flies up and down.

Two of the strange shadows cut through the rope that ties the horses to their stakes, the other two shadows slip under the tent, stand still, do not move, hear Daria's wail, throw themselves on her. One of the two presses her to the ground, holds his hand to her mouth, the other tears the clothes from her body, kisses her, licks her throat, squeezes her breast, licks her belly, satisfies his stinking greed. The other one watches, wipes the slobber from his mouth, opens his *shalvar*, rubs his manhood. The shadows swap places. It is the second one's turn. He presses his heavy body between Daria's legs. He is about to plunge his desire into Daria's body once again when Samira wakes up, knows there are strangers in the tent, knows they are with her mother, knows the strangers have not seen her. Samira reaches out to the side, her hand finds the sickle. The same sickle with which her mother cut her umbilical cord. Samira jumps, throws herself on to the back of the strange man, puts the sickle around his throat, screams and yells.

The stranger rears up to shake the weight from his back. Samira holds tightly on to the sickle so not to fall on to the floor. Samira hangs on to the sickle, feels how she is cutting the skin, the flesh, the throat of the stranger.

Only God knows that Samira has unintentionally, and in a moment shorter than it would take to say four short *be-isme-Allahs*, slit the man's throat and killed him.

Samira smells blood.

Daria rolls her dishonoured body aside, finds the rifle, shoots. Hits her target. The second strange man falls to the ground.

The two strange shadows who have untied the horses run into the tent. Their eyes are just getting used to the darkness, they are just hearing groans, they are just hearing the quick breaths of Daria and Samira and are about to leap on them when the light from an oil lamp falls upon them. The men from the other tents are standing before them, aiming their guns at them. No one speaks. None of the men moves. The world in the tent stands still. Still as death. Only blood is moving. Nothing else.

The man that Samira has unintentionally killed lies on

the ground. The sickle in his throat is a red gap, is a laughing mouth. Blood spurts from the rapist's throat. He lies still. With his *shalvar* around his knees. Everyone can see his manhood. It is limp, dangles lifelessly from his body. His manhood has lost its power.

The dead man's brothers stand there with their arms raised. The boy and the woman have killed our brothers, they say.

You are thieves, says Samira. You wanted to steal our horses.

My father is an important commander, says one of the brothers. He will take revenge on you. On you and your mother, on your people and your tribe.

You will atone for it, says his brother. By God, you will pay for it.

We are the ones who will avenge ourselves on you, says Samira. The men of our upland will ride into your plain and avenge the shame that you have brought upon us and our tribe.

Be quiet, boy, says Olfat the ugly. It is not your business to decide what will happen next in this case. It is the business of the adults and elders.

The men from the other tents lower their eyes, take their scarves from their shoulders, rearrange them, rustle the fabric, fall silent.

Samira falls silent.

Olfat the ugly acts as though he has already assumed command over the people and the upland. The self-appointed commander spits, says, bind the rogues and bring the dead from the tent. Gather together. We must hold a council.

This time no one says Samir should take part.

They gather without him and without Daria, they discuss the incident, send Olfat's eldest son as a representative. He stands in front of Samira and Daria, licks his lips, says, the *shura* has made its decision.

Daria, without protection and without honour lowers her eyes, knows she has lost. Lost everything. Some people never lose in life. Lose nothing. Others always lose. Lose everything.

Olfat's son cares nothing for Daria's lost honour, says, we will send you back with the dead and the two living sons to their father. It is your own fault. Had your mother become my wife, she would have been under my protection, and all of this would not have happened. If we do not hand you over, the father of the dead will come and avenge himself for the death of his sons. *Khalass* and *tamam*. That's all.

My father would never have handed any of you over to the enemy's knife, screams Samira. You, your brothers and your father are cowards.

Olfat's son draws his arm back, strikes Samira in the face. The force of his strike is so strong that Samira falls to the floor. She pulls herself back up, her face is bleeding, she wants to hurl herself on Olfat's son when he aims his rifle at her and says, just try it, I have a good mind to kill you.

Daria pulls her child to her, wipes the blood from her face with her dress. It is my fault, she says. Take me. Do with me what you will. Spare my child.

Samira looks at her mother, says, be quiet.

Daria falls silent.

You belong to them, the son of the self-appointed commander says, and leaves.

Daria knows what that means.

Samira knows what that means. They will force her mother to marry one of them.

They will discover that you are a girl, says Daria. They will force you too to marry one of them. They might sell us both.

Perhaps they will kill us, says Samira.

We must escape, says Daria.

I know, says Samira.

Samira knows she has to be Samir when they escape.

Daria gathers together as many of her possessions as she can pack on the backs of the horses. Samira tears her mother's dress to rags. The dress that the brothers tore from her mother's body. She wraps the rags around the horses' hooves so that no one can hear them. She knows that she can only take the horses, that she will have to leave behind the sheep and goats, the chickens and their provisions. She knows that she must leave behind the felt tent that gave her shelter in all the summers and winters that have come and gone since her mother pulled her out of her body. Samira packs the ammunition and her father's rifle, her own rifle, the sickle and the hatchet, ties it all to the horses' backs.

Samira strokes the soft noses of the horses, leads them close together, presses her body against the body of her father's stallion, stays as close to the horses as possible so that they are not afraid, so that they are still, so that their hooves are quiet.

I am frightened, says her mother.

Samira says nothing.

A Test

What sort of man is he? asks Samira.

Who? asks Daria.

My grandfather.

He is my father and he is your grandfather, says Daria.

Is he a good father and grandfather? asks Samira.

Daria laughs. What is a good grandfather and a good father?

Samira shrugs her shoulders. She does not say, my father was a good father. Instead she takes a stone, throws it, does not hit anything.

I don't even know if he still lives in our highlands, or if he is even still alive at all, says Daria.

At every mountain, in every valley, by every big tree, Samira asks, can you tell where we are? Do you recognise that rock? That peak?

No, says Daria.

When it is dark, Samira lights the fire, spreads out the blankets, fetches water if she finds any, puts the pot on the fire, takes the load from the backs of the horses, unpacks the dried whey and the old bread, when they have eaten she packs everything up again, lays the blanket around her mother's shoulders, lies down, looks into the sky and does not know whether they will ever arrive anywhere.

Daria sits by the fire, stares into the flames, falls silent. She does not even catch the bubbles that jump from the pot. Only when Samira is asleep does Daria start babbling. She babbles and babbles. Words that Samira does not know.

Poor Daria, who are you speaking to? Daria, Daria. Be careful, you have lost your mind, says the fire.

When did I lose my mind? asks Daria.

The fire does not reply.

I know, says Daria. I lost it in the tent. The day the second man drove his stinking desire into my body.

You are lying, says the fire. You lost your mind long before that. You have lost it because you overburdened yourself with guilt.

Leave me alone, says Daria, flaps her hand in the air as though a fly were flying in front of her face. Be quiet. You will wake my child with your chatter.

Poor Daria, says the fire.

Only when morning comes, only when the sun comes over the mountain, only when her child returns from the world of sleep into her mother's world, only then will the fire not talk to her any more. Only then will it calm around Daria. Only then will Daria be able to silence the madness in her head.

Why did you not sleep? the child asks her mother.

I was protecting us, says her mother.

We must get to a village. We have no flour and no bread, says Samira.

Daria pulls her little bag, embroidered with pearls, stones

and tiny bones, out from inside her clothes. I have money, she says.

That is not much, says Samira.

Samira and Daria walk and walk. Until their boots lose their soles. Until their feet are sore. Until their bones hurt.Until their souls are exhausted. In the next village Samira buys a pair of women's boots for her mother. A pair of men's boots for herself.

You should have brought your father's boots, says Daria.

I did bring them, says Samira. My feet are not big enough yet.

My child has small feet, Daria says to her fire in the night.

Your child is the only protection you have, says the fire.

Daria laughs. A laugh that she quickly loses again. A laugh that is crazy. Fine protection, says Daria. Her feet are too small for her father's big boots, and her strength is too small for the big world. Daria does not speak her words quietly. Not quietly enough that Samira does not hear them.

But I am protecting you, whispers Samira.

Fine protection, hisses Daria. Two men have stuck their stinking manhoods into my body. No, my child, you cannot protect us. You are not a boy. Not a real boy. You cannot replace your father.

Samira does not say, but I have protected you, does not say, the man would have killed you, would I have not slit his throat. Samira does not say it is my fault, I have committed a sin, blood is on my hands, I am a murderer and I did it for you so that you could live. Samira does not say she would rather be mute again.

Daria sees her child, comes to her senses, regrets her

words of stone. Regrets them too late. Her words are a red-hot, heavy stone, they land in her child's heart, build a nest there. They remain. For ever.

The days become birds, flock together, fly up and off. Her mother's words of stone remain. Samira no longer lays her head in her mother's lap.

Daria regrets too late, heaps blame upon herself. For ever.

Pull your scarf over your head, says Samira as they come closer to the next village. Samira speaks like her dead father. It is an order.

Her mother obeys.

On the way to the south of the country, Samira has been in many villages, but she has never seen as big a one as this. So many people, so much noise, so many cars, so much stench and so many eyes staring at them. A thousand and one pleasant smells lie in the air, traders and stall-keepers call out, shoo away cheeky children and fat flies with their rag dusters. Donkeys, oxen, horses, people get in each other's way.

Samira wants to ask her mother what the point is, where the good lies in having so many people living so close together. Samira does not ask, she needs all her strength to carry the stone in her heart.

She leads her little caravan into a quiet alleyway. From here she can see the whole of the bazaar up and down. Daria squats beside her daughter-son, says nothing, sees nothing. Only the pain in her child's eyes. Pain for which she bears the guilt. At the end of her long silence her mother says, forgive me.

Samira says, stay here. She speaks like her dead father. It is an order. Samira hangs her own rifle and that of her dead father over her shoulder.

What are you going to do with that? asks Daria.

Sell it and with the money buy a proper rifle so that I can protect you better.

Not your father's rifle. It is his legacy. His legacy for you, his son.

That's right, mother, says Samira, in a voice that sounds like her father's. This is my dead father's legacy for his son, who I am not. Samira shakes off her mother's hand, leaves her mother behind, goes. Like her father. With strong strides.

The man who sells Russian guns sits outside his little shop with his arms on his knees, chews on a little piece of wood. Samira with the two rifles strapped to her back, strolls past, walks to the other side of the road, knows the man has seen her, buys a loaf of bread, stuffs it under her vest, comes back, greets the gun-seller casually, not as though she wants something from him, squats in the sun casually, not as though she had sat near him deliberately, takes out her bread, tears off a piece, puts it in her mouth.

The man returns her greeting, casually, not showing that his curiosity has been aroused.

Only now does Samira notice how hungry she is. The dry bread sticks to her mouth, because she remembers her mother has no bread.

Nan bokhor, eat some bread, says Samira, tears off a piece, hands it to the gun-seller.

Offer a man a piece of your bread and he is not your enemy, the commander had said.

Tasha-kor, says the gun-seller. Where are you coming from?

From the mountains.

What are you doing here? asks the gun-seller.

I'm moving.

Where are you moving to?

To my grandfather's.

Are you on your own? asks the man.

No, my father and his men are waiting down there, by the entrance to your village.

Is the woman you came with your mother?

She is, says Samira. We are taking her to her father. She misses him.

The gun-seller narrows his eyes. Down there by the entrance to the village, you say?

Yes, says Samira, looks in the direction they have come from, nods, down there. She says it casually, acts as though she does not sense that the man has scented a lie and sees the boy and his mother as easy prey.

Who is your father? asks the gun-seller.

He is a commander, says Samira.

How many men does he have under his command?

Man che midanam, says Samira, shrugs her shoulders. She looks around the street, says, perhaps as many men as there are here.

As many as that? asks the gun-seller, raising his eyebrows. That is a lot.

If the enemy senses your fear, it makes him strong, her father had said. Lull him into a sense of security. If the enemy is frightened, he is dangerous. Give him the feeling that you are not afraid. Give him the feeling that he as well does not need to be afraid. Let him feel your strength, but do not frighten him.

But today my father has not brought all his men, says Samira.

The gun-seller nods, says, that is good. Because after all you are not going to war.

Is your village a safe place? asks Samira.

It is, says the gun-seller. No one here is afraid of anyone, only of the enemy.

As long as my father is here, you do not need to worry, says Samira. Takes the rifles from her shoulder, sets them down next to her, looks at the gun-seller, says *bebachshid*, have you got a sip of water?

The man points into the shop, there, go and get it.

Samira leaves the rifles lying there, casually, as though she were not afraid someone might steal them, goes into the shop, just stands there alertly with her eyes fixed on the rifles. She does not drink any water, comes out, says, you have got some fine weapons in your shop. I will tell my father, he might buy one of your Russian guns for me.

The gun-seller says, you already have two rifles, what do you want with a third one?

As she puts her rifles over her shoulder Samira laughs, says, we all have two rifles. But I'm the only one without a Kalashnikov. My father says now that I'm a real Mujahed he's going to get me one as soon as we get to the village.

Why do you not buy a Kalashnikov right now?

I have no money on me, says Samira. My father has the money.

Shame. A good deal should not be put off, says the gun-seller. How can I know that you will come back?

Only God knows that, says Samira.

The man says, at least have a look at your Kalashnikov.

I have no money, Samira says again.

Have you anything else that's valuable? What are you carrying on your horses? Lapis lazuli, gemstones, opium?

No. I have nothing. Just my two rifles.

They are fine rifles, says the man. Particularly the big one with the mother-of-pearl.

Yes, says Samira. It is beautiful and very precious. My grandfather gave it to me.

Bebinam. Let me see it. Sell it to me.

What do you want with it? asks Samira. It is beautiful, but it does not shoot very well and it takes a long time to load.

I'll sell it to the foreigners, says the gun-seller. They like old weapons, even if they do not fire any more.

What foreigners?

The Americans.

Samira does not ask, who are the Americans? Does not ask, why would they want to buy the old gun? Instead she says, why should I let you do the deal? I will sell my rifle to the foreigners myself.

The gun-seller runs his hand over the wood and the mother-of-pearl, scratches at it with his nail. As though, up there in your mountains, you will ever get to see any of those Americans face to face.

Bedeh. Give me it, says Samira, I've got to go, my father's waiting for me and my mother. She leaves the rest of the bread in the shop, casually, as though she were not hungry, as though her mother were not hungry, says, *be amane khoda*, may God protect you, goes back to her mother, takes the horses, leaves the village in the direction they came from. When they pass the shop with the guns again, she looks at the gun-seller, lays her hand on her chest, lowers her head, *be amane khoda*.

She has almost passed the shop when the gun-seller calls, *bache*.

Samira does not stop, says, as she walks on, *bogu*. Speak. What do you want?

Let us do an exchange, calls the gun-seller.

Samira leaves her mother and the horses where they are. What sort of an exchange?

A fine, new Kalashnikov for your old, worthless rifle.

No, thanks, says Samira, tightens her rifle-strap, makes as if to go.

Wait, says the man. Why not?

Because my grandfather gave it to me, and one day when I am a commander and a leader myself I am going to need it. Apart from that it is much more valuable than your Kalashnikov. I can get a Kalashnikov in any shop, in any village.

You should not put off a good deal, says the gun-seller.

For me this is not a good deal, says Samira.

What is a good deal for you? asks the gun-seller.

I want a gun and five boxes of ammunition. Make your mind up, my father is waiting, says Samira, and is almost believing herself that her father and his men are waiting for her at the entrance to the village. She straightens up, spits, tightens the rifles on her back, feels big and invincible. At the end of all their talking, the gun-seller feels as though it had been his idea to swap a Kalashnikov for the rifle. A Kalashnikov and five boxes of ammunition.

In parting, the gun-seller asks, do your father and his men have old guns like this as well?

Yes, says Samira.

Tell them to come to me, I will give them a good price for them.

Do you not feel sorry? her mother asks. It was your dead father's weapon.

My father is dead. I am alive, says Samira. And I want to stay alive. To protect us, I need a real weapon.

You speak harshly, says Daria.

Samira says nothing, shrugs, walks on, purposefully.

Daria is not used to walking along narrow alleyways with a scarf over her head and her face hidden. She stumbles, has to get out of the way of men, has trouble keeping pace with her child. When they are finally out of the village again, she squats on a stone, throws back her scarf, dries the sweat from her brow, says, I am afraid.

I have a good gun, says Samira. I will protect you.

I am not afraid of death, says Daria. I am afraid of losing you.

Samira does not reply. She whistles through her teeth, urges her mother and the horses on.

Who are you? asks a man who is also leading a little caravan.

I am Samir, the son of the famous commander.

The son of which commander? asks the man. Our country is full of all sorts of famous commanders.

The commander from the plain high up in the Hindu Kush.

What plain? Where abouts in the Hindu Kush?

The upland near the sea.

Samira falls silent, clicks her tongue, rides on, pulling the horses behind her.

Where are you riding to? asks the man.

We are riding to my grandfather's, says Samira.

Who is your grandfather? asks the man.

Samira does not want to leave herself exposed once again. She stops her father's stallion and her little caravan, straightens up and says cleverly: my grandfather? He is one of many grandfathers in our country.

What is your grandfather's name? asks the man.

Say his name is Mahfouz, says Daria. Quietly. So that the stranger does not hear her womanly voice.

My grandfather's name is Mahfouz, says Samira. Loudly, so that the stranger will hear her boyish voice.

Mahfouz? Mahfouz the barber?

Daria forgets to speak quietly so that the stranger does not hear her womanly voice. Yes, she says. Mahfouz the barber. That is my father.

Then you will be with him soon, says the man. You must pass high over that range between the two high peaks and you will reach a little village. There you can ask anyone. Everyone knows old Mahfouz who lives in the mountains above the village.

The man was telling the truth. At the end of four days and nights Samira and Daria see the little village. It is surrounded by fields with brightly coloured flowers growing in them, with the pretty name of *koknar*, poppies. A stream flows through the middle of the village. The people welcome Samira and her mother with great hospitality. They say, drink tea with us, share our bread, spend the night with us. They say, be careful, keep to the paths, beyond the planted fields everything is full of mines.

Daria recognises everything, the path into the mountains, the rocks, the curves and bends in the path, the peaks of the mountains, the plain, the view down into the valley, the tents. Daria even recognises some of the *kuchi*. Are you such and such, or so and so? she asks.

That's me. *Khosh amadi*, they say, welcoming Daria and her son.

Where is my father?

In his tent.

Mahfouz, Mahfouz, call the children, running on ahead.

Samira jumps from her horse, bows before her grand-father, kisses his hand.

Mahfouz is old and frail, and once while disabling a mine, he lost one arm but he says, thanks be to Allah, I am alive.

Samira likes her one-armed grandfather. He is friendly, and although age has made his eyes small, there is life in them when he looks at her. With his one arm he holds Samira so firmly that she feels as though she is being hugged by four.

Where are your other children? asks one-armed grand-father.

I have only this child, says Daria.

Thanks be to God, that child of yours is a boy. A strong boy. Where is his father?

Shahid shod.

Another one who has fallen victim to damned war, says one-armed grandfather.

Samira is surprised. She did not know war was damned. She had always thought war was good, because it had made her father a commander. She had thought war was impor-tant, because it made her father first into an invincible man, and then into a revered *shahid*.

Where are my brothers? asks Daria.

One-armed grandfather raises his arm, strikes himself on the head, weeps. Damned war has devoured them too.

Now you have a son again. A grandson, says Daria.

May God protect him, says one-armed grandfather.

I can protect myself, says Samira. I will protect us all. I have a weapon. I want to be a Mujahed.

No you do not, says one-armed grandfather.

Where is your arm? asks Samira.

The damned war stole it from me. A mine blew it to pieces. Our country is full of mines. You must be careful, or one of them will eat you up, too.

One-armed grandfather runs his hand over Samira's close-cropped head, asks, where is your hair?

Samira shrugs her shoulders.

What sort of style is that? asks one-armed grandfather. Who has shaved the boy's head?

Samira looks over at her mother, who is moving her lips without saying anything. Samira sees the words she is trying to say.

Daria finds her voice, says, I shaved it off. It is my fault. She says nothing more. Does not say, my son is not a boy, not a real boy. Does not say, Samir is to be Samira. She heaps more blame upon herself.

He is not a Talib, says one-armed grandfather. He is a boy of the mountain folk. He is a *kuchi*. A boy of the mountain folk wears his hair long. A *kuchi* shows the glory of his hair. Visible to one and all.

Samira likes the words of her one-armed grandfather. She likes the way he talks about her, calling her a boy of the mountain folk, a *kuchi*, and meaning her.

I am a *kuchi*, says Samira.

A real *kuchi* boy, says her one-armed grandfather.

One-armed grandfather tests his grandson's muscles, asks, are you strong?

I am, says Samira, bends her arms, tenses her muscles.

That is good, says her one-armed grandfather. Then show

me what all these muscles in your arms are good for. Come on, boy, take the things off the horses and take them into the tent.

I like you, says Samira.

I like you too, says one-armed grandfather and laughs.

For the first time in who knows how many days and nights, how many summers and winters, Samira laughs. It is a laugh that has forgotten the dead father, forgotten the rapists. A laugh that has forgotten that she has killed a man, that she had not provided enough protection. A laugh that has forgotten the word-stone in her heart. It is a laugh that is free, that is *azad*. A laugh that does not care whether it is Samira who laughs, or Samir.

A BREAKTHROUGH

Come, boy, says one-armed grandfather. We want to ride.

Where to? asks Samira.

Down into the village.

What are we going to do there?

We're going to trade skins, buy fat and tea and sugar, and we will take you to school.

What is school?

School is a place where lots of boys learn lots of new things.

I don't need school.

It's not your business to decide. If you do not go to school, what is going to become of you when you grow up?

I want to be like my father. Big and strong. Important and invincible.

You speak well. One-armed grandfather smiles, runs his hand over his grandson's head which is no longer quite as bald as it was, says, let us put off this useful talk until some point in the future. For the time being let us just go down into the village and do all the things I said. Agreed?

Agreed, says Samira. She always agrees. With everything the grandfather says.

All the way down into the village, Samira and her grandfather laugh. Samira gets off her horse, skips and dances around her one-armed grandfather as she has never done with anyone before. She is without worry or fear. More than she has ever before been in her small, yet big, life. She has even left her Russian gun in the tent because that was what her grandfather wished.

So? What is up? he asks. Do you miss your gun?

Samira smiles. No.

You see? says the grandfather. I knew it.

You always know everything, says Samira.

Do you like it here in your new home?

It's almost more beautiful here than it was in my own upland, says Samira, and is amazed at what she is saying.

For what reason is it almost more beautiful here?

Man che midanam, says Samira, shrugging her shoulders.

As in all the hours that they have been travelling, there is not a human soul to be seen, but Samira speaks quietly nonetheless. Because it is important what she has to say. She takes a deep breath, puts both hands to her mouth, goes very close to her grandfather's ear, says, I have to tell you a secret.

One-armed grandfather straightens up, smiles, says, but a secret is only a secret for as long as you keep it to yourself. One should not be careless with secrets.

Samira nods.

Think carefully about whether you want to give up your secret.

It is a terrible secret, says Samira, and does not want to

think, does not want to wait. Cannot wait. The secret bursts out of her. I have killed a man.

One-armed grandfather does not smile any more, stands in front of his grandchild, says nothing, looks at Samira. Samira stands as still as he does, feels the bitter aftertaste of the words that have freed themselves from her mouth.

One-armed grandfather bends down to his grandson, says, one who kills another human being also kills a part of himself. May God will that you never have to do it again.

Samira stops breathing.

Her grandfather sits down on a stone, gives his grandson a one-armed hug and says nothing more. Samira sits under her grandfather's one arm and weeps. Weeps. Weeps.

Her grandfather props his one arm on his thigh, gets to his feet and says, come. We have a long journey ahead of us. Everyone in the village knows one-armed grandfather. The important ones and the unimportant, the wealthy with good clothes and lots of cloth, and the poor clad in nothing but rags. Samira likes that. Her father was different. Her father only greeted the few important and wealthy people.

You know everyone, you are an important man, says Samira.

Everyone is important, says one-armed grandfather.

Samira nods. Although she does not know for what reason.

My father said there are important and unimportant people.

Every human being is created by God, says one-armed grandfather. For that reason alone each of us is important. Regardless of whether we are commanders or beggars, women or men.

Then I am important too, says Samira.

You are, says one-armed grandfather and laughs. And shall I tell you what else is important?

Samira puts her hand in the one hand of her one-armed grandfather, smiles, hops from one leg to the other, beams at the old man, shakes her head. Tell me.

Eating, says one-armed grandfather. It is important for people to eat. We will go to Hadji Mussa and eat as much of his delicious dal as we can get into our bellies.

Greetings, Hadji Mussa, says one-armed grandfather. This is my grandson. His father, God rest his soul, fell in the damned war. Now Samir is going to live with me. And just imagine, my grandson has never eaten dal in his life.

Khosh amadi, welcome, grandson of Mahfouz. The nice dal-seller transfers a decent-sized ladleful of his fragrant, hot dal to a bowl, places it in front of Samira, says, so here is the first dal of your life. Eat, my boy, and enjoy it, for you will not find better dal than this anywhere, neither in the mountains of the Hindu Kush nor anywhere else in the whole wide world.

Samira stuffs her face with rice and dal as though she has eaten nothing for four days. Her bowl is not even empty when the nice dal-seller gives her a new ladleful. Just eat, he says, so that you will be big and strong, so that you will turn into a real man and warrior.

Samira looks at Hadji Mussa, looks at her one-armed grandfather, smiles, says, my father wanted me to be a commander and go to war, but he is dead. Now I live with my grandfather, and he does not want me to kill men.

The nice dal-seller does not smile any longer, says, you are right. I spoke stupidly. For what reason should you be a warrior, kill and be killed? Enough warriors have come and gone, have been born and been killed. We have enough war. The nice dal-seller draws all the air around him into his body, blows it out along with all the dead and all the wars that have entered his soul, and laughs. Maybe when you're grown up you want to be the same as me, and be a dal-seller? What do you think of that?

It is the first time anyone has asked Samira what she wants to be when she's grown up. She does not know what to say, and thinks and thinks and searches her head for an answer.

Samira shrugs, says *man che midanam*, what do I know. It's true, she does not know. While she goes on filling her mouth with dal and rice, at the same time thinking about her job, while she looks now at her one-armed grandfather and now at the nice dal-seller, while Samira thinks and thinks and realises how little thinking she has done until the day she saw one-armed grandfather, far away in the sky a big silver bird quietly flies over the village.

The nice dal-seller stretches out his arm, points to the sky and says, there they are again. The foreigners who have come to free our homeland.

Samira and her full-of-dal mouth look at the sky, see the silver bird and all of a sudden she knows what answer she must give. *Pilot*, she says.

Pilot? asks the nice dal-seller.

Pilot? asks one-armed grandfather.

Bale, says Samira. *Pilot*.

You want to be *pilot*? That is an unusual job, says the nice dal-seller. At least for someone who lives here in the middle of the mountains of the Hindu Kush.

What's unusual about it? asks one-armed grandfather.

Well, says the nice dal-seller, I'm just an insignificant dal-seller, I live here in the middle of nowhere in the mountains and don't know much about the rest of the world and I don't know much about planes and pilots and flying either. But I know enough about that and about the rest of the world to know that if someone wants to be a pilot and fly a plane, if someone wants to do such an important job he must know foreigners, he must do a lot of travelling and he must learn lots and lots of things.

One-armed grandfather takes a sip of his tea, puts his little glass down on the table with so much power that it makes a bang, and asks, for what reason should my grandson not be able to do all that? Look at him, he's a bright, intelligent child. Then he will meet foreigners. Then he'll learn a lot, then he'll do a lot of travelling. Where's the problem? Do you think my grandson cannot do that? The moment we've eaten and drunk our tea, we'll make a start. It will be a long and arduous journey, but it will also be very beautiful.

Chi migi? What are you saying, Mahfouz, asks the nice dal-seller. What are your plans for your poor grandson? He has only just arrived, now you want to send him away again?

Samira stops chewing. The lump of dal sits heavy and dry in her mouth.

One-armed grandfather laughs, says, no, I do not want to send him anywhere. I am happy that he has come and I am not on my own any more. I will take him to school.

What? Where? asks the nice dal-seller. To school?

Bale. To school.

Samira opens her mouth, wants to say, I don't need school, I want to be a Mujahed, when it occurs to her that not long ago she had decided not to be a Mujahed and she falls silent.

Education is the gateway to the world, says one-armed grandfather.

How far is it to that gateway? thinks Samira. And what does that world look like? Are there wars there?

When they finally set off for the gateway to the world, Samira is no longer so sure whether her decision to believe everything her grandfather says and do everything he tells her was as clever as she thought.

This is my grandson, says one-armed grandfather, puts his hand on Samira's head, pushes her out from behind him, where she has hidden herself. Say hello to the teacher.

Salam, says the teacher, smiles and puts out his hand.

Samira likes the teacher. He is neither particularly tall nor particularly short, he has clean clothes, a scarf around his neck, he wears two little round panes of glass in front of his eyes held together by a wire which have the pretty name of *einak*, spectacles. The teacher smiles. Welcome, *khosh amadi*. Can you read and write?

Read and write? No, says Samira. What is that? I can ride and I am a good *buzkashi* player.

The kindly teacher laughs. That is good. Riding is important.

What is reading and writing? asks Samira.

Reading and writing? says the kindly teacher. That is the gateway to the world, and to life. It is the beginning of everything.

I ride my father's big stallion, says Samira.

The kindly teacher laughs. And what does your father ride when you're riding his stallion?

My father is dead, says Samira and smiles.

That's a pity, says the kindly teacher.

It doesn't matter, says Samira. I have lost my father and found my grandfather instead. My grandfather has lost his arm. A mine has torn it to pieces.

The kindly teacher runs his hand over Samira's head. And now he has you.

My grandfather says you will show me the world.

The world, says the kindly teacher and smiles. The world is a big place, full of wonder and surprises.

Show it to me.

I will, says the kindly teacher, laughs, puts out his hand.

At first Samira hesitates, then she decides to put her hand in the strange man's hand, goes with him, leaves her one-armed grandfather standing there. She reaches an empty square with just one tree, no field, no flowers.

This is our classroom, says the kindly teacher and goes with Samira into the little hut. On the floor there is an old kelim, with mats and cushions all around. Everywhere in the room there are neatly stacked things that Samira does not recognise. The room is so full of them that there is hardly room to walk or sit down.

What are those? she asks.

The kindly teacher smiles. Those, my boy, are my books. They are full of knowledge and words. The kindly teacher opens a book. Look, these are written words.

Samira is disappointed. This is supposed to be the world?

You are one who wants to see the world? says the kindly teacher. You go into the world with small steps. Word by word, book by book.

Samira looks at the kindly teacher, does not understand.

Look, he says, writes. S-a-m-i-r. That is your name.

That is my name? That looks nice, says Samira. Can you write everything?

Everything.

Write *Azadi*. Freedom. That is my horse's name. And it is a lovely word.

The kindly teacher writes. *A-z-a-d-i.*

Are there many people like you? asks Samira.

The kindly teacher laughs. Yes, he says. Very many. And you can become one of us. You just have to want it, you must be patient and practise a lot. And if you can read and write, you can write down all the pictures and words you have in your head, and other people can read them.

Samira shrugs. No, she says. No one shall see the pictures in my head.

Then do not write them down, says the kindly teacher. You just write what you would like to write. You yourself decide. You are *azad*.

Neither Samira nor the kindly teacher notices how long one-armed grandfather has been standing in the doorway watching them. That is beautiful, he says.

What is beautiful? asks Samira.

You two are, says one-armed grandfather, pointing with his one arm at his grandson and the teacher, sitting on the floor in the glow of the oil lamp, with all the books around them, and the pages of pictures and letters.

I have learned the words the teacher has taught me, says Samira on the way back into the mountains, talks and talks, and does not stop talking. The teacher told me about a great poet, he comes from Iran. That is a country. All countries have borders. We speak the same language. The teacher told me about our prophet. The prophet did not write the Koran himself, because he was like I am. Without education. Other people took his words and wrote them down. But by that time the prophet had been dead for fifty years. God does not like women. That is why he only made men prophets. We do not want a king in our homeland. People must learn to read and write, then they should decide for themselves how their life is to go. Samira talks and talks, hugs her grandfather, says, thank you. That is all she says, only a small, big Thank you.

So are you going to school? asks one-armed grandfather.

No, says Samira, in a voice that is clear and bright and full of happiness and contentment.

But. Her grandfather stops his horse. But I thought you liked it there.

How should I know whether I like school? asks Samira.

You just said you did, says one-armed grandfather.

No, says Samira. I do not want to go to school. I would rather go to the kindly teacher. I like it there, I like his books and all those words.

One-armed grandfather laughs. But that is school. He clicks his tongue, urges his horse, rides on.

I didn't know that, says Samira. I didn't know that the books and their words were school. If that is so, says Samira, and copies her one-armed grandfather, clicks her tongue, rides on, then I will go to school.

That is a clever decision, says the one-armed grandfather.

Tomorrow, says Samira. Tomorrow we will ride back down into the village and go to the teacher and his books and all those words.

No, my boy, says one-armed grandfather. We will not go. You will go. Along with the son of our Commander Rashid.

No, says Samira.

Why not?

I don't know the son of Commander Rashid.

Then you will get to know him.

I don't need to, says Samira.

Why not?

Because my father said I don't need any other people.

Everyone needs other people.

I am not like the other boys, says Samira.

That is true, says one-armed grandfather. Everyone is different from everyone else.

But I am very different from the rest of them, says Samira.

That is not important. You will get to know Bashir and you will ride with him, down to the village, to school. *Bass* and *khalass*.

AN ACCIDENT

Come, says one-armed grandfather. It is time for you to go to school. And today I will take you to Commander Rashid's tent in person, so that you and his son can ride to the village together and you do not have to go down into the valley on your own again.

Bashir is a funny name, says Samira.

It is not. It is a fine name, says one-armed grandfather. Bashir means the one with the good message, the intermediary, the messenger.

What good message does he bring? asks Samira.

Ask him yourself, says one-armed grandfather.

However much one-armed grandfather tries, his grand-child simply cannot be nice to Bashir. When Samira stands in front of him she asks, why don't you wear a shirt that isn't too big for you?

Bashir cannot defend himself. He looks at Samira, shrugs his narrow shoulders, says, *man che midanam*.

Samira becomes self-important and sounds like her grand-father. You should only say I don't know in reply to a question if you've thought about it and really don't know the answer.

Bashir looks at his father, looks at one-armed grand-father, looks at the new boy who seems to have come to the upland plain only to annoy him, shrugs again, leaves Samira standing there and disappears into his tent.

What sort of manners are those? asks one-armed grand-father. You do not treat a friend like that.

Commander Rashid strokes his beard, wants to put his arm around Samira's shoulder, she twists away and does not let him. At least your grandson is a real boy, says Commander Rashid. Take a look at my son. He is as thin as a twig and he walks through the world with his shoulders hunched. If he goes on like that he will never be a real man.

For the first time since she has known him, Samira feels sorry for skinny Bashir. She swings on to her father's stallion, whistles through her teeth, calls, come on, Bashir, we must get to school.

Can you only whistle so nicely yourself, or can you also teach my son how to do it? asks Commander Rashid.

I can teach him, says Samira.

Is that your stallion? asks Commander Rashid.

It is my dead father's, says Samira.

If you ever want to sell it, let me know. I'll give you a good price for it.

I'll never sell it, says Samira.

Bashir comes running out of his tent, pulling his vest over a smaller shirt that he has put on, runs around the tent, runs back into the tent, comes out, stuffs a book into his waist-coat pocket, comes back out in front of the tent. Samira cannot believe what she sees. Bashir is not sitting on a horse, he is sitting on a mule. A small, shaggy mule, with short legs.

What's that? asks Samira, is annoyed with herself when

she notices that her question gives the commander another opportunity to lay into his son again.

My son is afraid of horses, says Commander Rashid, tries to stroke Samira's stallion. The stallion pulls back its head, walks backwards, whinnies quietly. Who knows, says the commander, it is possible that you might be able to teach him to be a real boy.

Samira does not like Bashir. She has not liked him from the very first. It was easy for her to be horrible to him, and she enjoyed being self-important. But now she feels sorry for him. Samira does not like Bashir's father being so mean to him. He did not deserve that. On the way down to the village she stops repeatedly, rides slowly so that Bashir is not left too far behind her. He sits on his mule, holding the reins in one hand, in the other the book from which he is reading.

One does not read while riding, says Samira.

Bashir shrugs his shoulders, goes on reading.

Is your father always so mean to you? asks Samira.

Bashir looks up briefly, says, you don't have to talk to me, looks back at his book.

For four bends in the road, Samira and Bashir do not speak. Then Bashir briefly raises his head to say, and you don't have to pretend you like me.

Samira turns around to him, says, I am not doing that. I really don't like you.

Then everything's clear between us, says Bashir, goes on reading.

As he does every morning, the kindly teacher stands outside the school and greets the boys. When Samira and Bashir arrive, he smiles, says, *khob*, I see you have finally become friends.

Samira jumps down from her stallion. Bashir does not jump, he climbs down from his mule, hangs his head, walks on heavy feet, shakes hands with the kindly teacher, squats under the tree, hunches his shoulders, goes on reading his book.

Have you still not finished reading? asks Samira.

No.

Why not? asks Samira.

I will never finish reading, says Bashir, without looking at her.

Why are you here at all? asks Samira. I thought only boys who couldn't read came here.

Bashir does not look up, says, you're even stupider than I thought.

The kindly teacher calls over two boys, Madjid and Abdol-Sabour. Samir, from today you are not going to be taught on your own any more, from today you are going to go to class with the other boys.

I don't need the other boys.

Why not? asks the kindly teacher.

Because my father said so, says Samira.

Your father is dead, says the kindly teacher. God rest his soul.

Madjid and Abdol-Sabour stand there looking at their new schoolmate, leave him standing there and walk away.

Samira does not join the other boys in the class, goes to the room where she has been learning to read and write on her own until now, sits on the floor, takes a book, flicks through it.

Boy, says the kindly teacher. I said, from today you are to join the other boys.

Samira looks in the open book, concentrates on the dashes and curves.

The kindly teacher pushes her towards the other boys, makes her sit down on the floor, gives her a white sheet of paper, says to Khalil, who is sitting next to her, please show Samir how his name is written.

My name? You can write my name? asks Samira.

I can, says Khalil, wets his pencil with his tongue, bends low over his sheet of paper, reads each letter aloud as he writes it. S-a-m-i-r.

At first Samira holds the pencil as though it were her dagger, pressing down so hard that she tears the paper. Samira is so tense that her fingers, her hand, her whole arm, even her back hurt, and with all the effort and strength that she is putting into writing, her body becomes as hot and damp as if she had ridden twice the whole length of the plain.

The kindly teacher takes his pointer, stands in front of his pupils, reads words from the board, the boys speak after him. Mother. Father. Homeland. Freedom. Azad.

While Samira practises and writes, scratches and shreds the paper, repeats words and sweats, she observes the other boys and is amazed at how many of them are missing arms, legs and hands because they have stepped on mines.

I like the boys, says Samira to the kindly teacher, thinks for a moment, asks, why are there no girls here?

That is a long story. People think girls do not need to be able to read and write. They think girls are not as clever as boys. And because girls eventually turn into women, people think there is no point in girls going to school because they cannot use their knowledge later on anyway.

Samira looks at her teacher, her eyes alert and attentive. Do people speak the truth?

Many little wrinkles cross the kindly teacher's brow, he asks, what makes you ask about girls?

Samira shrugs.

Does the question have anything to do with something your father has said?

Samira shrugs.

My poor boy, says the kindly teacher. In a country such as ours, there is no easy answer to the question of girls and women.

Samira shrugs, does not dare look into her kindly teacher's eyes.

When the time finally comes for Samira and Bashir to go back up to the mountain, Bashir has disappeared. All the boys, even the one who has lost his legs to the mine, look for him and call to him. No one finds him.

Only when the kindly teacher calls, boy, you must go back to the mountain, your father is waiting for you, only then does Bashir come out of his hiding-place. He has tears in his eyes, sobs, buries his face in the jacket of the kindly teacher, says, Samir can do everything. And everyone likes him.

The kindly teacher presses the boy to him, says, no one can do everything.

My father wants me to be like he is, says Bashir, he wants Samir to be his son. He does not want me. Bashir sniffs back the water in his nose, wipes away his tears, looks at the floor.

The kindly teacher takes Bashir by the shoulders, looks into his tear-filled eyes, asks, did he say that?

Bashir shrugs.

Boy, says the teacher, go back up to your mountain, to your father. Do not be sad. I promise you, your father does not want another son. Samir is a good boy, but you are your father's son. His own flesh and blood. You are confused. I promise you, everything will be fine.

Bashir sniffs up the rest of the water in his nose, climbs on to his mule, sees Samira sitting on her stallion, straight-backed, full of joy and contentment.

Good, says Samira, then I will come back tomorrow.

That is good, says the kindly teacher. I will wait for you, for you and your friend Bashir. Samira draws as much air into her body as she can, pulls herself up, is about to say, he is not my friend, looks in the eyes of the kindly teacher, sees the eyes of poor, skinny Bashir, says, we will come.

That is good, says the kindly teacher.

I don't like him, says Samira to her mother and her one-armed grandfather.

For what reason do you not like him? asks her one-armed grandfather.

Because he is not a real boy, Samira says.

The days grow wings, become birds, flock together and fly away. Samira rides down into the valley, goes to school, learns what is to be learned, writes, reads, does sums, sits there with open ears and eyes and is constantly amazed at how much bigger the world is than she thought. She just thinks, I have finally understood the world, when she discovers that there are still things that she does not know, does not understand.

I like this village better than the other one, says Samira.

Why? asks Daria, amazed at how little of Samira still remains in her daughter-son.

Because it is bigger, says Samira, putting a piece of bread and yoghurt in her mouth.

For what reason is a village that is bigger better than a smaller one? asks Daria, amazed at how much of the little child still remains in her Samir, even though he is almost as big as she herself is.

Man che midanam, says Samira.

You should not say that, says one-armed grandfather. You should only say I don't know as the answer to a question if you've thought about it and really do not know the answer.

I like this village better, says Samira, because no one knows me here. Because I am new to the people.

One-armed grandfather raises his eyebrows, wants to say something but cannot get it out, because Samira is quicker than he is.

Man che midanam, says Samira, smiles. Cheekily, and full of courage.

One-armed grandfather smiles, picks up a stone, acts as though he wants to throw it at her.

Samira shrieks, jumps to her feet, throws herself on her one-armed grandfather, says, *man che midanam*. I have thought about it, she says. There is no answer to that question in my head.

The days come and go, Samira and Bashir ride down to the valley together, to the village, to school, they eat together, they are in the same class, but Samira and skinny Bashir simply do not want to like one another.

He can't ride, says Samira. He can't play *buzkashi*. He is skinny, he can't shoot. He can't do this. He can't do that. He can't do anything.

He can read, says the kindly teacher.

He is so rough, says Bashir. He is without a heart. He is stupid. All he can do is go dashing round the place on stupid horses. All he can do is ride, shoot, hunt and climb up and down the mountains.

Tell him to teach you, says the kindly teacher. You will see, all those things can bring happiness.

Every morning and every evening it is the same game. Samira rides off ahead on her stallion, Bashir trots along behind on his mule, sees nothing and nobody, keeps his eyes on his book.

Read to me, says Samira. She is not asking skinny Bashir. It is an order.

I can't read when I am sitting on the mule, says Bashir. It wobbles from side to side too much.

What? So why do you pretend to read?

So I don't have to see you, says Bashir.

Samira stops her stallion, waits until Bashir has caught up with her, looks at him, says, you are a liar.

I am not, says Bashir, draws back his arm, is about to hit Samira with his book, the stallion is startled, lifts its head, rears up on its hind legs, comes back down, slips, stumbles. The path is narrow and steep, the stallion takes a big step sideways, slips, Samira cannot stay on its back, falls, tumbles, rolls. She somersaults down the first slope, slips past a dry bush, cuts her arm and neck so that the blood flows, goes on somersaulting, bashes her head, looks like a sack of onions skipping down the mountain. Stones break away, go hopping and flying in front and behind of Samira. She has the taste of blood in her mouth, pains in her belly, in her arms, in her legs, in her whole body. She comes to a stop. Lifelessly. A flat stone the size of a loaf skips down after her, lands on her belly. Stays there.

The stallion gets to her first, prods at her with its soft nose, nibbles at her ear, whinnies quietly. Bashir and his mule take longer to wind their way down the narrow path.

Bashir wails and cries as though he were the one who was injured and in pain. He climbs down from his mule, almost falls because his knees are trembling so much that they can barely hold his skinny body. Bashir kneels beside Samira, touches her, shakes and shakes her. Samir. Samir. I didn't mean to do that. I didn't mean to push you down the mountain. Wake up. But however much Bashir wails and cries, Samira does not move, just lies there. With the stone on her belly, with her mouth open, eyes shut. Covered with blood. With a fat wound right above her eye. Damp and red, the slit gapes open like a laughing mouth.

I didn't mean to kill you, says Bashir, puts his hand on the stone that lies on Samira's belly, feels his hand moving. Slightly. Very slightly, his hand moves up and down. Let him live, says skinny Bashir. Dear God, ruler over the world and everything else, let him live and I promise I will do good, I promise I will be nice to him, serve him and do whatever he wants of me.

Bashir lifts the stone, carefully, as though it were part of Samira's body, sets it aside. He bends down over Samira, puts his ear to her mouth, hears her breath, smells the scent of her skin, touches her lip with his ear. Bashir runs his hand over Samira's head, its hair longer now, sees a tear fall from his eye on to Samira's lips, stay there. Bashir does not know why he does what he does, he is wide awake, more wide awake than he has ever been before, he stays where he is, bending over Samira, looks at her face, sees her mouth, kisses it.

All this time Bashir holds his book firmly in his hand, and

does not let go of it. After the kiss, Bashir does not know what to do next, he only knows he is not strong enough to heave Samir on to one of the animals. He puts his hand on her chest, opens his book, says, you told me to read. So I will read.

Bashir reads until Samira coughs, opens her eyes, puts her hand on Bashir's, says, you kissed me.

Bashir gives a jump, stops reading, says, I was reading.

But first you kissed me, says Samira, opens her eyes, breathes heavily, says, I am frightened.

It is my fault, says Bashir.

Hold me, says Samira, claws her hand into his shoulder, and with his help manages to get on to the back of the mule.

Samira is bent forward, she can hardly breathe, closes her eyes, opens them again when she hears voices, when she is lying down, when she feels hands finding her wounds and her aching body, when water is trickled into her mouth.

Samira recognises the voice. It is the voice of the kindly teacher, she wants to smile, cannot, opens her eyes, sees the people around her only as brightly coloured patches with no beginning and no end, they blur into one another, wave their arms wildly around, put their heads on her chest, want to hear her breath. Samira sees the tree she is lying under, sees the invisible listener who squats on the branch above her, looks down at her, smiles.

He kissed you, says the invisible listener.

I know, says Samira.

Was it nice? asks the invisible listener.

It was, says Samira.

He is speaking, says the kindly teacher, that is a good sign.

Will I die? asks Samira.

Do you want to die? asks the invisible listener.

Samira shrugs.

The butcher who has been bent over her, pressing and examining her belly to see if anything within her is torn, gives a start, says, the boy is in pain. He has internal injuries, we must not move him. The butcher knows what he is talking about. In the many years of the wars that have come and gone, he has seen many dead and injured people, has saved them, has lost them.

I want to live, says Samira, lets her head fall to one side, loses the last bit of colour in her face.

You are not going to die, says the kindly teacher. The mullah is here, he has brought his medicine. The butcher is here, he will stitch your wounds, he will make you well. You are not going to die, boy. Do not go. Stay here.

The butcher puts his hands on top of each other, lays them on Samira's chest, presses down, lets go. I learned that from the Americans, he says. Back when they helped us in our battle against the Russians. With this method you can save anyone's life, however dead they might be. The butcher snorts and sweats, presses, lets go, presses, lets go, until colour returns to Samira's face. The butcher wipes his brow with a rag stained with the blood of the cow he has just slaughtered, says, there, you have your pupil back. The butcher feels half like the American doctor who taught him how to save lives, half like the warrior he wants Samir to become. I have given him a new life, he says. We shall see whether he deserved it, and whether he will become a warrior.

This boy is already a warrior, says the kindly teacher. He is a fighter. He has spent his whole little life fighting.

Where is Bashir? asks Samir.

I thought you did not like him, says the invisible listener.
Where is he? asks Samira.

I am here, says Bashir, sniffing the water up his nose.

Samira does not see Bashir, does not hear his voice, does not open her eyes, does not hear or see anything or anyone. Not even the invisible listener squatting on the branch.

The sun goes away, the other boys and the butcher go away, the stars come, gleam bright and cold, call to Samira.

You will see, says the kindly teacher, and runs his hand over Bashir's head, he will be well again. Samir is a brave, strong boy. He will not die so quickly.

But all his blood is running out of his head, says Bashir. He says it quietly. Quietly. Because he does not want what he says to be true.

The sun comes up, casts its warmth and its light into the village, wakes everyone and everything, including Samira. She opens one eye. Only one eye. The other is swollen, crusted, full of blood. Samira looks to one side, sees Bashir, speaks quietly so that no one else can hear her. Bashir, open your eyes. Read to me from your book.

Skinny Bashir reaches out beside him, finds his book, opens it, reads. Quietly. So that only Samira can hear.

In the middle of his reading Bashir stops. I want to give you a present to make your pain go away quickly, he says, reaches under his blanket and takes out a little wooden flute.

Samira puts the flute to her mouth, blows, makes a sound, closes her eyes, says, go on reading, sleeps until her one-armed grandfather comes.

Why has my mother not come? asks Samira.

Boy. What are you thinking? The place is full of strange men.

I want to see her, says Samira.

I will tell her you're well.

I am not well, says Samira. I want my mother. I have something important to tell her.

Tell it to me, says one-armed grandfather. I will tell her.

Samira knows her mother will be dying a thousand and one deaths because she does not know, because she cannot know whether the men have found the girl in her. Samira swallows down tears, reaches out her hand, lays it on her one-armed grandfather's one arm, says, tell my mother her son is alive, tell her that her son will protect her. Tell my mother her son has found a friend.

I will tell her, says Samira's one-armed grandfather, taking Bashir by the hand, he says, boy, come, we're going back to the mountain. Your father's waiting for you.

I am staying here, says skinny Bashir, tell my father I am going to stay down here in the village for as long as Samir has to stay here. Skinny Bashir speaks with a voice that is not quiet. A voice that is new, a voice that has found courage.

Samira likes Bashir's new voice, she likes it when her grandfather comes to visit her, likes it when the other boys come and gather under the tree, just for her, likes it when they laugh, when she can laugh herself, likes her little presents. Samira likes it that she likes Bashir and the other boys.

For what reason are you good to me? asks Samira.

Why should we not be good to you? asks Majid. You are one of us.

How do you know that? asks Samira.

My father told me, says Majid. He said, today you help

someone, tomorrow you might need help yourself, then others will help you.

Samira smiles, does not say, my father said I don't need other boys.

A thousand stars shine in the dark sky, there is no moon to dim their brilliance. Stars are the lights of God and the dead, says Samira.

I have no dead, says Bashir. If I were in charge, I would give you another present. Bashir speaks quietly so that no one hears, not even God, only Samira. I would ask God to swap my father for yours. Then my father would be dead and yours would still be alive.

I do not want that, says Samira.

But I do not want you to be sad, says Bashir.

I am not, says Samira, amazed because until that moment she did not know that her life was without grief, that she likes her new life, life without her father. Samira points to the sky, says, there. That is the star that God shines for my dead father.

Which one? asks skinny Bashir, following Samira's finger.

That one, the bright one just there, says Samira, laughs, no, it is the other one, the smaller one. Or perhaps that one back there, the big one with the ring. What difference does it make? asks Samira, answers her own question. None at all. It makes no difference. Because it is not true. Because it is a lie. No star shines for my father.

Perhaps no star does shine for your father, but it would be nice if you could believe that one was shining for him, and this way he was with you, says skinny Bashir.

Samira does not say, I am happy that he is not with me, she says, you are a dreamer.

What is wrong with dreaming? asks skinny Bashir.

Dreaming, says Samira, is for girls, not for men and boys. At least not real boys.

Skinny Bashir turns on his side, looks at his friend, runs his finger along the cut above his eye, says, your heart is hard. As hard as the scab that has formed over your wound.

Samira says nothing, lies there without moving, enjoying his touch.

You are my best friend, says Bashir, thinks, then says, you are my only friend.

I want to be your friend for as long as you need me, says Samira. And I will always be with you.

Tell me your secrets, says Bashir.

You should not be careless with secrets, says Samira.

I will not tell anyone, says Bashir.

I have no secret at the moment, Samira lies. But if I do have one, I will tell you.

The days and nights under the tree come and go and soon become Before. Those are the nights when Samira and Bashir talk and talk, hold hands, gaze into each other's eyes, go to sleep side by side. Those are the nights when the kindly teacher sits beside the boys, opens his book, reads stories about lovers, about heroes, about princesses and kings, about swans and witches. Those are the nights when the pages of the books flutter quietly in the wind, carry their fairy-tales into the world.

At first you were enemies, says the kindly teacher, now you are like Leili and Majnun.

Who are Leili and Majnun?

They are lovers. A girl and a boy.

Skinny Bashir puts his hand to his mouth to hide his laughter. Samira keeps silent, says nothing. The kindly teacher turns round, closes his eyes, sees his Leili. His lost Leili.

Life is winning, life is losing, says the invisible listener. Quietly. So that no one hears.

A GIRL PROSTITUTE

My breasts are getting bigger and bigger, says Samira. Quietly. Because what she has to say is important. Because it is not easy for her. Samira is filled with *sharm*. She lowers her eyes, sees her mother uncomprehendingly and prays to God that her mother may find a little reason and that she may have an answer for her.

Daria looks at her daughter-son, with eyes that are awake. What do you want to do? asks Daria.

If I knew what I wanted to do, I wouldn't ask you, says Samira.

The decision is easy, says her mother. Go out and look at the life that you and the men lead. And then look at me and look at the life that I and the other women lead.

Why did God not send me into the world as a real boy in the first place? asks Samira.

My poor child, says Daria. Why do you torment yourself with questions to which you will not find an answer? For what reason did God send wars and call your father to him? Why did he take my honour? Why does he allow men to knock their wive's teeth out? Why did he take my reason?

Why did he take your grandfather's arm? What rational reason is there for him to take arms, legs, mouths and futures from children? God does not give answers to questions.

Daria squats by her fire, lets the bubbles jump, does not catch them. She says, God made you as you are. The rest is up to you. You are not a child any more. It is up to you to make yourself the person you want to be. Everyone must do what is best for themselves. If you want to live your life as Samira, find a way. If you want to live your life as Samir, find a way to do that. Daria turns to the simmering, scolding water, catches a bubble. Then Daria does what is best for her. She disappears inside herself. To the place where there are no questions, no answers, no reason.

Samira does something she has not done in a long time. She goes to her mother, kisses her on the forehead and strokes her hair. Daria looks at Samira, smiles, remains sitting by her fire, hums a melody. She catches some bubbles that jump out of the pot, saves them, does not catch others, lets them die, with a hiss.

Samira swings on to her stallion, holds the jewelled and jangling reins loosely in her hand, rides. Just like that, with no purpose, without haste.

In the distance Samira hears the cheerful singing, the trilling and drumming of the girls and women. They are celebrating the *Hadji*'s wedding. The *Hadji* is taking a wife. A new wife, Firouza. Firouza has been on God's earth for just as many summers and winters as Samira. Firouza is lucky. She is a girl. A real girl. She has found a husband. The *Hadji* will give her her own tent. He will send his second wife, along with her children, into the tent of his first wife and her children. The *Hadji* will spend the nights with Firouza. She is lucky. She will be the *Hadji*'s new favourite wife.

Samira understands enough about the lives of women to know the day will come when Firouza too will not be the *Hadji*'s favourite wife any more. Just as the day came when the *Hadji*'s first wife, and then his second wife, were no longer his favourites. But today Firouza is lucky.

Hadji, say the other men, as they laugh and smooth their beards. *Hadji*, you're a sly fox.

The *Hadji* wants to be a sly fox. He wants wives who are young and beautiful, who, with their youth and beauty will make him young and satisfy his lust.

Everyone must do what is best for himself.

The *Hadji*'s father chose his first wife for him. After she had pulled many children, living and dead, out of her body she became fat and ugly. So the *Hadji* took a new, young wife. A very young wife.

People said, the *Hadji* has a good heart, he has taken a little orphan as his wife. He has given her a home, protection and security. The *Hadji* does not tell the men that it was not generosity. That his second wife, the little orphan girl, had been a prostitute before he brought her up to the mountain and made her his wife. He does not tell the men that he only took the girl prostitute because she had confused his senses, robbed him of his reason. The *Hadji* says none of this to the other men.

All this, the girl prostitute tells Samira.

While the *Hadji* sits on the carpet outside his bride's tent, the other men are full of envy. They imagine the joy that will be the *Hadji*'s when he is alone with his third young bride. Firouza does not understand what her mother means when she says, your husband will make you a woman tonight. The other women trill and sing for Firouza's happiness. While all this is happening, the *Hadji*'s second wife, the former girl prostitute, beckons Samira into her tent, to take her as her confidante. Though forbidden, Samira goes.

I have no choice, says the former girl prostitute, I must confide in someone. Who knows, perhaps one day I will be too costly and too burdensome for the *Hadji*, and he will want to get rid of me. Then at least there will be one person on this damned earth who knows my story, and will demand that he do right by my children.

The *Hadji* wants to kill you? asks Samira.

Who knows, says the former girl prostitute.

Why are you telling me of all people? asks Samira.

Because I see you have a great secret yourself. One who has a secret himself can be trusted to guard the secrets of others, says the former girl prostitute.

I will not reveal my secret to you, says Samira.

The former girl prostitute laughs, puts her hand on Samira's arm, says, I do not want to know. My own secrets keep me busy enough.

Samira can see in the former girl prostitute's eyes that she is not lying. Samira knows what she is doing is forbidden. A woman, especially a woman who belongs to another man, has no business talking to a stranger, especially if that man is unmarried, and she is telling him a secret.

The decision is easy, her mother had said. Take a look at the life that I and the other women lead.

Speak, says Samira. I am listening. Your secret will be stored safely with me. I will put it in the place where I store my own secret.

So listen, says the former girl prostitute. It happened on

a day when everything was as it always is. The *Hadji* is in a battle. At one point the enemy is shooting. At another point the *Hadji* and his men shoot back. At one point the enemy advances, at another point the *Hadji* and his men advance. At the end of all the shooting the men return to their camps, which are not far from one another, light a fire, eat, drink, pray. Anyone who wants to relieve himself or do anything else climbs on to the mountain and hides between the rocks.

The *Hadji* looks for a nice little nook and does what he has to do. When he is about to go back down to his men, he hears someone very close by, apparently doing the same thing as himself. The *Hadji* creeps up, sees the other man, puts his gun to his head and waits, because the other man quickly has to pull up his *shalvar* and drop his *kamiz*.

Do you want to hear how the story continues? asks the former girl prostitute.

Samira nods, says, *bogu*.

Then you will have to come closer, says the former girl prostitute, so that I can talk quietly.

Samira obeys.

The former girl prostitute goes on talking. It turns out that the other man is an enemy, and also a *Hadji*. Neither of the men really likes to go to war. They do not like to kill, least of all another *Hadji*. After a lot of talking, the enemy *Hadji* makes my *Hadji* an offer. He says, I will give you a present if you give me my life.

Samira asks, how do you know all this?

I know it from my *Hadji*. He himself told me, says the former girl prostitute, takes her child, which has been hanging from her breast, turns it round and puts the other breast between its tiny lips.

Samira knows she should not look. She is half a man yet she knows there is no shame in looking. She is a woman, she has breasts herself.

Shall I go on? asks the former girl prostitute.

That is up to you, says Samira.

The former girl prostitute continues. The enemy-*Hadji* speaks in the loveliest colours, the loveliest pictures and scents, of a girl who is as tender and fresh as the bud of a flower with the morning dew upon it. At the end of his story, which is full of sighing and lip-licking, the enemy-*Hadji* says, give me my life and I will give you this girl as a gift. The *Hadji* agrees, is brought to the girl's hut and sees that the enemy-*Hadji* was not lying. Before him stands the loveliest thing that the *Hadji*'s eyes have ever seen.

Samira swallows, says, you are the girl that the enemy-*Hadji* gave to your *Hadji*.

I am, says the former girl prostitute.

Even though she does not know whether the story of the former girl prostitute is true, Samira says, tell me more.

The enemy-*Hadji* wanted me for himself. But he lived in the same village as I did, and everyone knew I was a prostitute.

Samira does not ask what a prostitute is. The former girl prostitute can see in her eyes that she does not know. A prostitute, she tells Samira, is a woman who sells her body to men. Every woman who is alone and without possessions, who has no husband and protector, must sell her body so that she does not starve.

Samira does not ask what selling your body means.

The poor enemy-*Hadji* does not feel guilty for not taking me as his wife, because if he had he would have lost his reputation and his respect among the people, says the former girl prostitute, and breathes so heavily that her breast slips out of her child's mouth and she has to put it back in.

My *Hadji* has said that he will look after me, but I could see in his eyes that he is lying. He did not want to take me with him and protect me, he just wanted me to satisfy his lust. But I was cunning. I devised a ploy to win his protection.

Samira can not imagine that a man would fall for a woman's cunning.

The former girl prostitute laughs, says, I know my way around you men, I know what you like. I spoke to *Hadji* in a voice that was full of sweetness, of warmth, that crept into the *Hadji*'s ears, tickled and stroked him. I laid the sweet sound of my words on the *Hadji*'s heart and numbed every clear thought that he had in his head. I stood before the *Hadji*, drew my arms back, pushed my breasts towards him, told him to follow me, went into my hut and gave him everything he desired, everything he dreamed of.

Samira swallows and stays silent.

The former girl prostitute lowers her eyes, then opens them wide, and throws Samira into ever greater confusion with a glance that is filled with lust.

I see it clearly, says the former girl prostitute. It is the same lust, the same fire, that burns inside you. Samira can not bear to look at the girl prostitute any longer, and lowers her eyes.

I pushed the *Hadji* on to my blankets, leant down to him, revealing my breasts, which were young and firm, sat in his lap until he groaned, until he sighed, says the former girl prostitute. She closes her eyes, and leans her head back, then says only then did I ask the *Hadji* whether he would take me with him, look after me and protect me.

Samira swallows, does not know the reason she is breathing so quickly.

I demanded from the *Hadji*, says the former girl prostitute, that he swear to protect me. Without thinking, the *Hadji* said, I will take you with me. I will look after you and protect you. You belong to me. Only when he swore on the life of his sons did I finally satisfy his lust. The former girl prostitute leans back, puts her child to the side, opens her thighs, does not pull her skirt down, does not cover her breasts, takes the tips of her naked breasts between her fingers, rubs them, licks her finger, and says, I do that so that they do not hurt after my child has been suckling on them.

Samira knows only that whatever the reason for all this nipple-rubbing and finger-licking might be, the former girl prostitute should wait until Samira is no longer in her tent.

The former girl prostitute sees the confusion in Samira's eyes, goes on rubbing the tips of her breasts, says, if the *Hadji* throws me out now that he is taking a new wife, or if his first wife throws me out of his tent and I have no one to protect me, will you look after me?

Samira does not know what to say, does not know where to look, does not know what to do. She does not know why the blood is surging through her body, why breathing is so difficult, why all the images, thoughts and words in her head are tumbling around. Samira opens her mouth, says, I'm not a . . . She says nothing more than that. Instead she jumps up, runs out of the tent, wants to ride off, just wants to get away. No matter where to. Then a hand grips the reins of her stallion. Samira immediately knows it is the *Hadji*.

Hey, Samir. Boy, he says. This won't do. You can't just

disappear. Come with me. Don't you know that today is my wedding? Come, boy, you are my guest. I have slaughtered my fattest goat.

Samira smiles, shoves her heels into the belly of the stallion, so that it dances uneasily on its legs, lifts its head, and wants to free itself from the strange man's grip and ride off, when Commander Rashid appears, followed by Bashir. They all block her path.

You're not trying to get away? says Commander Rashid.

No, says Samira, smiles.

The *Hadji* lays his arm around Samira's shoulder, pushes her to the carpet in the grass, where men are already sitting, smoking water-pipes, eating fruit, cracking pistachios, chatting loudly, laughing and singing.

Samira sees and hears all that as though she is far away, up on the peak of the mountain. The only thing that Samira sees clearly is the bare breasts of the former girl prostitute. The only thought that has room in her head is the question of how it can be that she liked what she saw. She herself is half a woman, has breasts that are getting bigger, that push and strain.

The decision is easy, her mother said. Look at the life that you and the men lead, and then look at the life that I and the other women lead. Samira wanted clarity, yet now she is more confused than she has ever been in her life.

Bring incense, calls the *Hadji*.

Incense is healthy, her mother always says. It protects against disaster and illness. It drives away flies, lice and fleas, drives away the evil eye, envy and disfavour. Samira inhales the smoke as deeply as she can, keeps it in her body as long as she can, so that it drives away the images she would rather not have seen.

The thin clouds of smoke float around Samira, settle on her face, on her hair, creep through her clothes, settle on her skin. For days, when the smell from her clothes creeps into her nose, she will see only one thing: the bare breasts of the former girl prostitute, her spread thighs, her tongue licking her lips.

May the *Hadji* have a long life, calls one of the men. It is the father of Firouza, the girl who is going to become the *Hadji*'s third wife tonight. Four cheers for the *Hadji*, says the man. He does not smile.

He has nothing to smile about, says Bashir. Quietly. Because no one is to hear it but Samira. Bashir tells Samira that Firouza's father had debts with the *Hadji*. Debts that he could not pay. And then the *Hadji* said he would let him off his debts if he gave him his daughter as a wife.

Samira looks at Bashir, says nothing, hoping that she is not about to hear another story that will make her head spin.

What can you give me instead? the *Hadji* asked him generously, knowing full well that the poor man had long since sold everything he had ever possessed.

How do you know that? asks Samira.

I was there, says Bashir, and he lowers his eyes. He speaks even more quietly, says, I was in the tent with the *Hadji*'s second wife and heard it.

The orphan girl that he brought up on to the mountain? asks Samira. What were you doing there? Were you alone there?

No. What are you thinking of? They would have shot me if they had found out. I was there with my sister Gol-Sar.

Bashir lowers his voice still further, and says, Firouza's father begged and pleaded for a postponement, but the

Hadji would not budge. He said, if you cannot pay I will take your daughter. My other two wives are not fresh any more. It is good for me to get an oven-fresh wife.

Did he really say oven-fresh? asks Samira. Fresh from the oven, like a loaf of bread?

Yes, says Bashir. I heard it with my own ears.

Firouza's father kissed the *Hadji*'s feet, pleaded with him and said, my daughter is still a child. But the *Hadji* did not listen to him, said, either you pay the money or you give me your daughter.

Samira looks at Bashir. You are not lying, are you?

No, says Bashir. On my sister's life, I am telling the truth.

Poor Firouza, says Samira. Even more quietly, she asks, what did the *Hadji*'s second wife have to say about all that?

Bashir likes the fact that he and Samir discuss things that are so important. He likes the fact that the other boys and men see that Samir and he are really good friends. Bashir looks around the men, speaks quietly and behind his hand, says, the second wife said that the *Hadji* has not been a real man for a long time. She said, he cannot satisfy a woman, and that he has never satisfied her. And she said she will avenge herself on him, or perhaps even find someone who would kill the *Hadji* for her if he dared not to feed her and her children.

Samira feels dizzy. She wants to find someone to kill the *Hadji* for her?

The darker it gets, the more the stars show themselves, the louder the men become, the more wildly they beat their drums, the more passionately they clap their hands, the more they sing uncontrollably. The men eat, drink and dance until the *Hadji* gets to his feet, and, laughing and slobbering, goes to his young bride's tent and all the other women come out.

Samira uses all the coming and going to slip away. She disappears. She rides off, feels the wind in her hair, whistles through her teeth, urges her stallion to ride on even faster, the stallion breathes heavily, snorts, its hide becomes warm and damp until it is flying.

The dark of night is pleasant and calming. No shrill colours or sharp edges, no loud cries and questions. No stories of old men taking a second or a third wife, no bare breasts of a former girl prostitute, no Firouza who does not know what it means to be turned from a girl to a woman. Samira flies, floats through the night, asks her amulet to help her, gives all images and words, all thoughts and fears to the wind to carry away and deposit somewhere on the remote peak of a high mountain. Just do not carry my thoughts and images to my dead father, thinks Samira, and rides even faster.

At the way in and out of the plain, where the path down to the valley begins and ends, Samira climbs up the mountain above the path, sits on a rock that is as black and smooth as her father's rock was, stretches out, notices how the strength returns to her body, how her breath becomes calm and even, her heart beats in time with the star that winks and shines above her as though it had come only to please her. Samira closes her eyes, a light breeze stirs and the angels come, lift up Samira, lift her into the sky until she floats on her own, flies. Past the stars, past the moon, past the sun, to where even God no longer is, where there is Nothing, where Everything is.

Hey, Samir. Are you asleep?

For a moment Samira does not know which world she is in, where the voice is coming from, who it belongs to, then she recognises it. It is Bashir's sister. Gol-Sar stands at the foot of the rock, looks up at Samira. Her thin cloth and wide skirts catch the breeze, flutter.

What are you doing here? asks Samira. She jumps down, as though she were weightless, and asks, has something happened?

No, nothing has happened, says Gol-Sar. Quietly. Breathes the words. Eyes lowered.

Samira looks straight at Gol-Sar, as though she had not heard the whispered words.

I saw you today, says Gol-Sar.

Samira is just wondering why Gol-Sar is saying that, because after all they see each other many times every day, when Gol-Sar lays her hand on Samira's arm and looks at her. Looks her straight in the eyes. These two things, laying the hand on her arm and looking straight into her eyes, would not be so bad if it were not the middle of the night, if they were not both alone, far from everyone and everything. Not if Samira were not Samir but Samira, and she did not like the hand on her arm. But she does like it, it is warm and pleasant. Samira gives a start, pulls back her arm and asks, what reason have you to be here?

I often come here, says Gol-Sar.

In the middle of the night? All on your own?

Gol-Sar smiles, takes the scarf from her head, puts it on the ground, squats down, looks up at Samira, says, it is good to be alone, it is good not to have anyone saying, do this, do that. This is the only time and the only place where I can be free. Gol-Sar leans back, lies down on her scarf, spreads out her arms, looks into the sky.

Samira does not know why she does what she does, but she does it. She holds out her hand to Gol-Sar, says, come with me. As though Gol-Sar had been waiting for that and for nothing else, she takes Samira's hand, holds it tightly, follows her.

Samira helps Gol-Sar up on to the rock, spreads out her *patu*, lies down on her back, pulls Gol-Sar down to her. The girl-boy and the girl lie side by side, gaze into the sky with its thousand and one stars and say nothing.

A soft, warm snake comes into Samira's belly, tickles her, presses its nose against her heart. Gently. Without pain. Samira's heart is full of happiness, when she sees Gol-Sar. She does not know what is happening to her, more than that she does not want to know. She closes her eyes, asks the happiness-snake to stay. Gol-Sar does not move, does not look at Samira, asks, Samir, do you like me?

Samira asks the happiness-snake not to go.

Gol-Sar does not move, breathes deeply and calmly. She is not touching Samira, but it is still as though she had wrapped her arm around Samira, as though she had laid her head on her breast.

I like you, says Samira. Just as I like your brother, just as I like the other boys in the village. Yes, says Samira, I like you.

Do you like the *Hadji*'s second wife as well? asks Gol-Sar.

The happiness-snake disappears, leaves a cold, empty place in Samira's belly.

I saw you earlier, says Gol-Sar.

What did you see? asks Samira.

I saw that you were in her tent, says Gol-Sar.

Samira thinks, lies, says, the *Hadji* told me to bring wood to his wife. I did that.

Nothing more?

Nothing more, says Samira, turning to face Gol-Sar. Samira runs her finger over Gol-Sar's forehead, takes a curl, wraps it round her finger, smiles, plays with the curl. Nothing more.

That is good, says Gol-Sar, and smiles.

Samira lets go of Gol-Sar's curl, lies on her back, says, if your father or your brother see us here, they will shoot us both.

They will, says Gol-Sar.

Then again perhaps they would not, says Samira. If they knew that things are not as they seem, if they knew the truth, the whole truth, they would shoot only me.

If they shoot you, I want them to shoot me too, says Gol-Sar.

Samira rests her head on her hand, looks at Gol-Sar, thinks. Thinks for a long time, then says, you do not understand.

Because I am a girl? asks Gol-Sar. That is not fair. You must know that girls understand much more than you men think.

I know that, says Samira, leans forward, almost touches Gol-Sar's lips with her own. Almost. Samira looks at Gol-Sar for a long time, says, your hair smells of rosewater.

I hear the beating of your heart, says Gol-Sar.

Your eyes are as beautiful as the eyes of a young deer, says Samira.

Let them shoot us, says Gol-Sar. Let them. I am prepared to die.

Gol-Sar does as Samira did, takes one of Samira's curls, wraps it round her finger, strokes it, plays with it.

Have you lost your mind? asks the invisible listener, squats down on Samira's hip, looks at her with his eyes wide.

Samira stops smelling the scent of rosewater in Gol-Sar's hair, stops seeing her, stops hearing her heart.

What do you do all day? Samira asks Gol-Sar, trying to drive away the invisible listener, to drive away the happiness-snake, to drive away the softness and the breath of Gol-Sar, to drive away the caress of the breeze.

What? asks Gol-Sar, wakes up from her dream, wakes up from her forbidden longing, from her failed desires, from her failed wishes.

When you get up in the morning, what do you do? asks Samira.

This is a question that no one has ever asked me before, says Gol-Sar. She thinks, says, Nothing. I don't do anything.

Nothing? asks Samira. That's impossible. Everyone does something when they wake up in the morning.

I light the fire, says Gol-Sar.

And then?

Nothing, says Gol-Sar, laughs.

Come on. So you get up, you light the fire, and then . . .?

Then I go to the stream and fetch water.

And then?

Then I put the pot on the fire, and wake my younger brothers and sisters. Then I wash them, give them tea if we have any. Then I knead the dough, bake bread, go to the stream, wash the clothes, sweep out the tent, take the goats to the meadow.

That is a lovely life, says Samira.

It is not lovely, says Gol-Sar. It is a life full of Nothing.

That is not Nothing, says Samira.

Yes it is. I wish I was a boy. You have a good life. You are outside all day. You can do whatever you want. I envy you and my brother. You go hunting, you go into the village, you go to school, play *buzkashi*, shoot your guns. You will go to war and defend our homeland against the enemy. You negotiate with other men, you trade and buy goods. The lives of boys are important, exciting. The life of a girl is a punishment.

Maybe that is so, says Samira.

It is as I say, says Gol-Sar. We have no responsibility in life, we do Nothing. And one day, when some man comes along and marries us, we have children and again we do nothing, again we have no responsibility.

It is not easy to bear responsibility, says Samira. It is not easy to earn bread for the family.

Do you think it is easy to see my brother being able to do whatever he wants? He does Everything. Yet I am allowed to do Nothing. Look at me, says Gol-Sar.

Samira looks at her, wants to touch her, wants to stroke her. She does not know why she wants this. She does not do it.

Am I not a human being? asks Gol-Sar. Does the same blood not flow through my veins as flows through my brother's veins? What is different about me?

You are beautiful, says Samira, looking into Gol-Sar's dark eyes, which are full of fury. Full of fire.

That is all we are. We are beautiful. Nothing more. Until the day a man comes and takes us as his wife. After that we are not even beautiful any more.

What sort of words are those? asks Samira. How do all these dark, heavy thoughts get into your beautiful head?

Gol-Sar hesitates, says, from my brother.

Bashir tells you these things? How does he know all that?

From his books, says Gol-Sar.

I did not know that thoughts like that could be found in books, says Samira. I thought books only had stories of heroes, kings and princes.

I will tell you a secret, says Gol-Sar and laughs.

Samira does not know whether she wants to hear another secret.

I can read, says Gol-Sar. Bashir teaches me. Secretly. He teaches me everything he learns.

You can read? asks Samira. I thought girls . . . Samira does not go on. Says that is good. Girls should learn to read and write.

Do you like me anyway? asks Gol-Sar.

Samira lies down on her back, smiles, says, I like you. In fact I like you even more than you can think.

You don't know how much I can think, says Gol-Sar. It is possible that I can think more than you can imagine.

Samira the girl-boy laughs.

Gol-Sar the girl laughs, says, they will shoot us.

Let them, says Samira. As long as we live, we live. When we die, we are dead. What are you doing tomorrow?

The same as every other day, says Gol-Sar. Nothing. The only change is that I am going to see poor Firouza.

Why is Firouza poor? asks Samira.

Because she is still a child, says Gol-Sar. It will be two summers more before she is *balegh*.

Samira wants to ask what *balegh* means. Does not ask.

My mother says the poor thing will be in pain. That's why she is poor, says Gol-Sar. Perhaps right now, in this very moment, as you and I lie here, gazing into the sky, being free, she is being made into a woman. By a man who stinks, who has no teeth, who is four or five times as old as she is, is even older than her own father. That is why poor Firouza is poor. She is poor because she is a girl.

Poor Firouza, says Samira.

And tomorrow I am going to see her and take down all the

beautiful things that have been hanging in her tent, and give them back to the *Hadji*'s first wife.

What kind of beautiful things?

The marriage hangings, says Gol-Sar. The red-yellow-green woollen threads hanging on the entrance to the tent, to protect her against the evil eye and evil spirits. The brightly coloured embroideries, the jewellery and the long strips of carpet, the glittering cloths and clay bowls in which we burned the incense. I am going to fetch all of those things because the *Hadji* only borrowed them.

But the men say she has a good life, because she has a tent all to herself, says Samira.

That is what the men say, says Gol-Sar. Do you want to hear the truth?

Samira does not know whether she wants to hear the truth.

The *Hadji* only puts her up in his own tent for one reason. He does it because he wants to satisfy his lust on the poor child unhindered, undisturbed by anybody.

Samira falls silent. She does not know why she is breathing heavily.

When her mother dyed her poor girl's hands and feet with henna and said to her daughter, it is so that your bride's blood won't overheat, she wept. Poor Firouza did not understand anything, she just wept along with her mother, says Gol-Sar, and wipes tears from her eyes.

Samira does not ask why the bride's blood should not overheat, sees Gol-Sar's tears, swallows down her own tears, does not know why they are coming.

Poor Firouza, says Samira.

Now I have made you sad, says Gol-Sar. That was not my intention.

It doesn't matter, says Samira.

You see, says Gol-Sar. The life of boys is good and exciting, meaningful, important. The life of girls is a punishment.

Maybe that is so, says Samira.

A Set of Steps

Bashir lies beside his friend on the rock, gazes into the sky that is full of stars and listens to the melody that Samira is playing on her flute. A heavy, sad melody.

Even your songs are sad, says Bashir. What is making you so melancholy?

Samira sighs. Nothing. Everything.

You still owe me a secret, says Bashir.

The day to tell you has not yet come. Until then my secret remains somewhere in the mountains of the Hindu Kush, under the stone where I put it.

Bashir touches the scar above Samira's eye, says, I will find your stone. I will walk up and down the Hindu Kush and study every stone on every path I take. I will wander for so long until I find it. I will see it and know, it is the stone under which my friend has laid his secret. I will greet the stone, kiss it. I will not look under it, will come to you, sit in front of you and wait. Wait until you yourself tell me what your secret is.

I am lucky, says Samira. Very lucky. Because I have a friend like you.

You have always been lucky, says Bashir. Your whole life has always been full of luck. And your greatest luck was to have a father like yours.

Samira pays no attention to her friend's words, goes on playing her flute.

You had a father who respected you, says Bashir. You owe him your strength, your power, Everything. You owe it all to him, and to the respect he gave you.

You are mistaken. My father did not respect me. He respected no one, not even himself, says Samira without looking at Bashir and goes on playing her flute. Then she stops playing, says, he did not feel like a real man, because he brought only one child, only me, into the world.

Why did he not take a second wife? asks Bashir. Then he could have had many children.

Samira laughs. A bitter laugh. Poor Bashir, she says. The world is not as simple as you think. My mother was not the problem, my father was.

Bashir does not understand.

A man shot my father's testicles, says Samira. His testicles and his manhood.

Your father was a man without testicles and manhood? asks Bashir. So it is your father's fault that God did not give him more sons in his life? I thought that if a man did not have enough sons and children it was always the woman's fault.

On the one hand Samira wants to laugh, but on the other, she wants to cry when she says, there are more men like my father, men who have no testicles and no manhood.

Bashir does not believe Samira. You mean there are men with no . . . Bashir does not go on.

Who have no manhood, who are not real men, says Samira, finishes what her friend does not dare say.

Bashir smiles, and says in return, the one son your father put in this world is stronger and more powerful than most of the boys and men I know. I wish God had made me like you. I would be the happiest man on earth if I was you.

Samira laughs. A bitter laugh. You don't know what you are saying. No man wants to be like me.

Someone who is like you can not know how it feels to be someone like me, says Bashir. Look at me. I can not protect anyone. I can not fight anyone. My father says I am a weakling. He says I am as dried up as a scrawny chicken. He says it would have been better if my mother had pulled me out of her body as a girl right away.

Your father, my father. We should forget our fathers, says Samira, in a voice that is as hard as the scar that has formed over the wound above her eye.

The only thing my father likes about me, says Bashir, is the fact that I have you as my friend.

Samira plays her flute, then does not play it, says, you think God or my father or whoever else created me, made me the person I am? You think it is God's will and work to make a real boy out of me? That is not true. Whatever I am, or am not, I myself made me.

Bashir wants to say something, does not dare speak against his friend's intense fury.

Whether a person is strong, can ride, can play *buzkashi*, can fire a gun and hit the target, is not God's work.

I have come to terms with how I am, says Bashir. Some men are like you and others are like me. Men are not all the same.

That is true, says Samira. Some men are different. So

different that you have no idea how different they are.

We must live with it, says Bashir. Some things are as they are, and cannot be changed.

Who said that? asks Samira. Where is that written?

Bashir laughs. Only a few summers ago you could neither read nor write, and now you ask me where that is written.

Yes, says Samira. Who says we must live with things as they are? Things can be changed. Even my mother, who has lost all her reason, knows that. One can learn, one can fight.

I don't want to fight. I don't want war, says Bashir. I want a life in peace.

My poor friend, says Samira. Life is a fight. And fighting is life. All that I am, all the things that I can do, I am and can do only because I have fought. You remember? In the beginning I used to hold my pencil the way I hold my dagger. But I did not give up, I fought, I practised over and over until I learned to write. The first time I saw the kindly teacher I didn't even know there was such a thing.

Such a thing as what? asks Bashir.

As reading and writing, says Samira.

I don't believe that, says Bashir. You are lying just to make me feel better.

No, says Samira. Someone like you cannot possibly know how it feels to be someone who is like me. For me, every word that I write or read is still a struggle. When you read, the birds are shamed into silence by the sound of your voice. When you write it looks like a dance, as your hand skips and hovers over the paper like a bird hopping from branch to branch, with no apparent effort.

You speak beautifully, says Bashir. Your words are like a delicate rose petal settling on my heart.

Stop that. You are embarrassing me, says Samira. She

closes her eyes, does not understand the reason her body is shaking. The same shaking as before, when, easy as a cat, she jumped from her father's rock. She sees herself running through the darkness to the peak of the mountain, stands before the sun, spreads out her arms, breaks the light of the sun, casts a shadow into the valley, on to the rock, on to her father, until the sun rises and Samira carries it on her hands.

Where are you? asks Bashir, though he knows his friend is in the world of dreams.

Samira says, first I saw myself lay the rose petal on your heart, then I climbed to the peak of the mountain and vanquished the sun.

Bashir laughs. Lies down on his back, says, you speak like a poet. Tell me the story of the girl and the calf.

You know it, says Samira and laughs into the sky.

I know it, says Bashir, but you shall tell it to me.

So listen, says Samira and begins.

The king with the lovely name of Bahrame Gour is a good hunter. On a peaceful day that God gives him he goes hunting. He is accompanied by his men, his vassals and his slaves, his vizier and a girl with a beautiful face and the body of a gazelle. Her silky, shining hair is long, her dark almond eyes are two jewels, her skin is as tender as a peach. The girl moves with the grace of a wild cat, her singing makes the birds fall silent. She plays a little harp. The melody that she draws from her instrument brings joy to the hearts of all who hear it.

The king looks at her and says, I admire your voice and the skill with which you play your instrument. Tell me, beautiful girl, do you also admire my strength and my courage?

The girl keeps silent, and her silence pierces the king's heart like an arrow.

The king is very unhappy, and asks, what must your lord and master do to win your admiration for his courage and his strength?

At that moment a deer appears.

The girl says, if you possess enough strength to pin the foot of this animal to its head, then you will have my admiration.

The king throws a marble at the animal's ear. When it scratches its ear with its foot, the king fires his arrow and hits. Now do I have your admiration for my strength and might?

Your deeds deserve no admiration, she says. If a person practises the same thing over and over again, his success is guaranteed. Your success is not the result of your strength and your courage, but the result of practice and experience.

The girl's brazenness so infuriates the king that he orders his vizier to take her away and kill her. The girl persuades the vizier to spare her life and take her to his own palace, far from the king. The girl has a plan. She sees a newborn calf, puts it over her shoulder and carries it up the sixty steps to the entrance of the palace. She does that every day that God gives her. And even when the calf is a fully grown cow, the beautiful girl still carries it up the sixty steps to the palace.

In that way the girl becomes stronger and stronger, and more and more beautiful. Finally she gives the vizier her earrings and her jewellery, asks him to buy meat, fruit, nuts and other such things and invite the king. The vizier undertakes to pay for the meal himself, spreads out his most precious carpets at the top of the sixty steps, prepares a rich meal and asks the king to be his guest.

The king climbs up the sixty steps and says, vizier, you have built yourself a fine palace, but when you are old, how will you climb these exhausting steps?

The vizier says, my king, whether I can climb these steps lies in the hands of God, but allow me to show you something.

The girl has put on her finest clothes and hidden her face beneath a scarf. She puts the cow over her shoulder, climbs the steps, sets the cow down and says, you have seen it, my king, I have carried this cow up sixty steps with my own strength. Tell me now, my king and master, is there a man with strength enough to carry the cow back down again?

That is not a question of strength, says the king. You must have carried the cow up the steps since it was a small, light calf. So you can still do it today, because it is a matter of experience and practice.

But when you pinned an animal's foot to its head with your arrow, you said it was the result of your strength and your courage. Now I have proved to you that you were wrong. The young woman takes off her scarf and shows the king her face.

The king recognises her, is glad that she is alive and says, if this house has become your prison, then I ask your forgiveness. He rewards his vizier handsomely, takes the young woman away and marries her.

Did they live happily ever after? asks Bashir.

They did, says Samira.

Bashir straightens up, says, *khob*. Then I will practise, take one small step each day until I am the son my father wants me to be.

No, says Samira, and strikes the rock with the flat of her hand, so that Bashir, the mule and the stallion are startled.

Why not? asks Bashir. I thought that was what you expected of me.

No, says Samira. A big, heavy No. A No that disturbs the silence of the night and the mountains. A No that scares away the delicate rose petal from Bashir's heart.

It does not count, what I want of you, says Samira. It does not count what your father wants of you. All that counts is what you want, says Samira.

I want to be your friend. Nothing else, says Bashir, leans over Samira, looks into her eyes, hesitates, kisses her on the cheek.

Samira just lies there, she sees the face of her friend above her own, does not know what to do or say, feels his breath, hears his heart, which beats just as fast as her own.

Samira just wants to push her friend away, just wants to sit up, jump down from the rock, when Bashir holds her face and kisses her for a second time. This time he kisses her full on the mouth, sits up, turns his back on Samira, says, so now you know. Now you know what I want.

Samira is startled. She sits quietly, thinking, considering. Finally she decides to act as though Bashir had not kissed her. Neither the first time nor the second time.

What question did you ask when I told you the story? she asks.

Skinny Bashir shrugs his skinny shoulders.

You asked me if the king and the girl lived happily ever after.

And you answered that they did, says Bashir. For what reason do you ask?

Because this is a big question, says Samira. An important

question. The question of all questions. Because that is all that matters in a person's life. Happiness.

How do you know that? asks Bashir.

I know because I have seen my mother lose all her reason, I have seen my father lose his dignity, because they did not listen to their hearts, only ever did what other people, religion, tradition, the mullah and whoever else expected of them.

Bashir does not swallow down his tears, lets his friend see them.

I know from my own experience, says Samira, because as long as we live we have the strength to make whatever we want from our life.

Bashir shrugs his shoulders.

Samira puts her hand on Bashir's shoulder, summons all her courage, says, do you think a girl can have as much strength as a boy? Walk like a boy? Go to school, go to the bazaar, strike deals, haggle, spit, fight, sit with men in the tea-house, hunt, play *buzkashi*, do all that and everything else like a boy, like a real boy, even though she is a girl?

What? What do you mean by that? Bashir's voice is loud and shrill. Are you saying I'm a girl? He jumps from the rock and disappears into the darkness.

A MISSION

God rest his soul, says Daria, your father was a bright man.

No, he was not, says Samira.

Daria says, the commander was a man whose life was full of joy.

No, it was not, says Samira.

Do not speak of a dead man like that, says Daria. He was your father.

There is nothing I can do about that.

You are insolent.

Boys are allowed to be insolent, says Samira. You yourselves are responsible for that. Samira leans back, sips colourless tea, without sugar that tastes more of water than tea, looks at her mother who has lost all reason, says, you of all people are telling me what is right and what is not.

You are ungrateful, says Daria.

What have I got to be grateful about? Samira puts down her tea-glass, stands up, takes her *patu*, leaves her mother sitting in the tent, goes. At the entrance she turns around to her mother again, looks at her, wants to say something else. Does not say it. Falls silent.

My poor child, Daria says to herself, because there is no one else there who she can say it to.

What is wrong with you? asks Bashir.

What could be wrong? Nothing. Samira jumps from the stallion, picks up a stone, throws it. Just like that. Without hitting anyone or anything. It is Nothing. My mother has lost all reason. My father is dead. My grandfather has lost his arm. We have no animals, no money, no wheat, no skins. My tea is water and winter is not far off. What could be wrong? Samira looks at her friend, says, it is nothing.

Bashir does not know what to say.

Come, says Samira, pulls her friend along behind her by his sleeve, says, you know nothing about any of this. Let's play.

Leave me alone. I don't want to, says Bashir

Samira knows Bashir will follow her. Samira says, Bashir do this and he does it, she says, do that, and he does that. Bashir you are not strong enough yet, you cannot ride fast enough yet, you cannot wedge the dead calf firmly enough under your thigh, you make it too easy for the animal to get away from you, you must practise more, train more. You must get more strength in your arms and legs. Bashir, we will run up the mountain, we will run a race. Whatever Samira says, Bashir does it, because he wants to be like Samir.

Come now, says Samira. Stop behaving like a girl.

Bashir does something he has never done before. He grits his teeth, clenches his fists, takes a jump, throws himself on Samira, pulls her to the ground, throws punches. Samira was not expecting that. She takes a few blows before she understands what is happening. She grabs Bashir by the shoulder, wants to push him away. But Bashir remains on her chest, punching wildly at Samira. At the end of all the rolling about and being on top and being on the bottom and punching and being punched, they both lie exhausted on the ground, breathing heavily. They gaze into the sky, laugh, until a shadow falls across them.

Commander Rashid stands over them, laughs, says, well then. My son is not a fragile little flower. He reaches out one hand to Samira and the other to Bashir, helps them both on to their feet, looks at Samira, says, my boy, I thank you. You have made a real boy out of my son. I am in your debt. Tell me your wish and I will fulfil it.

Samira is still out of breath, is still startled by Bashir's wildness, yet she does not think for long, says, I need work. Real work with which I can earn money. The commander laughs, says, work? What sort of work could I offer you?

I am good with horses, says Samira. Almost as good as my dead father.

And what use is it to me that you are good with horses?

I can train them and break them in for the game. I have seen you in the game, I know where your weaknesses lie. I can help you.

You? Commander Rashid does not laugh any more. Boy. Be careful what you say. You take yourself too seriously. Have you forgotten who I am?

No, says Samira.

What gives you the right to think that I, the commander of this upland plain, could learn anything from you, from a boy?

Bashir stands there, looks from his friend to his father, wipes the sweat and blood from his face with his *kamiz*, still cannot believe what has just happened. He, skinny Bashir, has had a fight. Not with anyone. He has had a fight with the strongest, the most powerful of all the boys, brave Samir. Samir, the one all the other boys fear and respect.

He can do it, says Bashir, not knowing where he has got the courage to stand up and speak against his father.

Commander Rashid darts a look at his son and Samira, a look that is full of fury, spits, turns around, leaves them both standing there, and goes.

Samira swings on to her horse, says, I am riding to the village.

What will you do there? asks Bashir.

I will look for work, says Samira.

I am coming with you, says Bashir. He disappears behind the tent, comes back, sitting not on his mule as he usually is, but on a real horse. All the way down into the valley Samira stays close beside him, takes care to ensure that Bashir and his horse do not slide down the mountain. All the way down Samira explains to Bashir how best to arrange himself to feel safe on a horse. Sit upright, press your legs to its body, don't hold the reins so high, keep them loose, don't be afraid, stay on the saddle, your horse knows where it is supposed to go. At the beginning of the journey Bashir looks like a sack of onions that is not quite full, he wobbles and shakes, totters and slips, and threatens to fall off the horse's back at any moment. By the end of the journey Bashir is sitting upright, with his feet firmly in the stirrups, his thighs tight against his horse's body. By the time they ride into the village, Bashir is smiling, his horse is walking with its head held high.

Samira and Bashir ride once down the busy bazaar street and once back up it again, look at every shop and every stall, greet the men, the nice dal-seller, the butcher, the disgusting vegetable-seller, dismount from their horses, beat the dust of the journey from their clothes, stand there and don't know what to do next.

I'm hungry, says Samira.

I thought you wanted to look for work, says Bashir.

I don't know how to do that.

So what have we come here for? asks Bashir.

Samira scrapes the sand with her feet, looks at Bashir, shrugs, says, I must do something. Am I supposed to wait until all the money and all the provisions are used up, until we are all dead? Come now, we will go to the nice dal-seller and eat as much dal with rice as we can get into our bellies.

What's up, boy? asks the nice dal-seller. You look miserable.

I am, says Samira, stuffing a piece of bread with dal into her mouth. I must go to war.

Bashir, who is sitting next to Samir on the narrow wooden bench, cannot believe what he is hearing. You have kept that quiet, he says. You have lied to me.

I haven't, says Samira. It has just occurred to me. It is the only way.

The only way to what? asks the nice dal-seller.

The only way to earn money and help my family survive through the winter.

Boy, war is dangerous, says a disgusting vegetable-seller, as he gathers up his *kamiz* and his *patu*, and squeezes himself on to the bench on the other side next to Samira. He calls for a bowl of dal without looking at the nice dal-seller.

The nice dal-seller frowns, looks at the disgusting vegetable-seller, says, you are hungry today, my friend, you have just eaten three bowls of dal and rice.

Sometimes you are hungry, sometimes you are not, says the disgusting vegetable-seller, licks his lips, goes on staring at Samira and Bashir, says, for a second time, war is dangerous.

I need money, says Samira, as she edges away from the disgusting vegetable-seller.

There are other ways you could earn money, says the disgusting vegetable-seller.

I know no other way.

The disgusting vegetable-seller looks at the boys, licks his dal-smeared fingers, says, come and see me, I know a way. He throws a bundle of banknotes on to the nice dal-seller's cart, says, take what my dal costs, the rest belongs to the boy.

Boy, says the nice dal-seller. Quietly. So that no one else hears it, only Samira. Don't do it. Listen to me. Stay away from him.

A little snake enters Samira's belly. She does not know what kind of snake it is. She watches the disgusting vegetable-seller leave, then stuffs the banknotes into her waistcoat pocket and says, I must do it.

When Samira and Bashir reach the shop of the disgusting vegetable-seller, they can see even from a long way off that the man is lying on a sack of onions, that despite the heat he has wrapped himself up in his *patu*, his eyes closed and is breathing heavily.

Bashir grabs Samira by the sleeve, pulls her on to the other side of the street, where they creep among the chicken-seller's cart and cages. They both crouch there and watch the disgusting vegetable-seller moving his hand violently under his *patu*. Up and down, down and up.

What's he doing? asks Samira. Quietly. Because she thinks it's better if no one else hears.

Bashir is surprised, and whispers, stop being so prissy. All boys and men do it.

Do what? asks Samira.

You idiot, says Bashir. He's rubbing his cock.

What?

Bashir holds his hand in front of his mouth. He's rubbing his cock.

Samira cannot believe what her friend is saying. She narrows her eyes, looks over at the disgusting vegetable-seller, who is moving his hand more and more violently under his *patu*, looks at Bashir and asks, why is he rubbing his . . . ? Samira doesn't say the word.

Because it's nice, says Bashir, even more amazed. Don't you do it?

Samira does not know what to say. How should she know what cock-rubbing is, and that it is nice. Of course I do. It's just that I . . . oh leave me alone. Samira turns away so that she does not have to see the disgusting vegetable-seller any more, sees him anyway and does not say anything more.

At the end of all the rubbing and rocking and tugging, the disgusting vegetable-seller sits up and smiles, even though there is no one there to smile at, strokes his beard smooth and slurps tea.

Do you know where the butcher Hadji Soltan has his shop? asks the disgusting vegetable-seller when Samira and Bashir finally come over to him.

Samira does not speak, she just nods, her eyes wide open.

Tell Hadji Soltan I am sending you. Tell him the honoured vegetable-seller wishes to ask if his goods have arrived, and then tell him his parcel is with me, he can bring his stuff and collect my stuff. Understood?

Samira nods. *Bale.*

So? What's wrong? Why are you still standing around? The disgusting vegetable-seller puts his hand on Samira's back, pushes her to make her go.

Samira and Bashir want to go when he takes Bashir by the arm, says, not you, my boy. You stay with me. Come. He pats the sack of potatoes next to him, says, sit down.

No, says Bashir. I'm going too.

What do I get for this? asks Samira.

So you think you're clever? asks the disgusting vegetable-seller. You've had your money. Forgotten already? That was a lot of money, and you have many more things to do for me before you get any more.

And why did you not bring my goods straight away? asks the butcher when Samira gets there.

Samira thinks, says, the vegetable-seller probably thinks I would steal the goods and run off with them.

And is he right?

No.

I believe you, says the butcher. After all, I saved your life and you owe me something. Here are the goods for the vegetable-seller, tell him to give you mine and then you bring them here. Understood?

I didn't expect him to trust you, says the disgusting vegetable-seller, taking the little package, stowing it in the back corner of his shop between green vegetables and fat aubergines. He, in turn, takes out another small package, gives it to Samira and says, go. Bring it to him.

What else must I do to earn the money you gave me? asks Samira when she comes back from the butcher.

Not so hasty, says the disgusting vegetable-seller. Come here and sit with me, I'll tell you what you can do for me.

But first I need to know you a bit better. You and your little friend here. I must know whether I can trust you. What is that lovely *ta-vis* you're wearing around your neck?

He tries to touch it. Samira pulls away.

It goes on like that for a while; the disgusting vegetable-seller asks this and that and tries to touch Samira, and then Bashir. The boys keep pulling away. Finally, the disgusting vegetable-seller says *khob*. Come to me tonight, I will tell you what you must do for me.

Tonight? That is not possible, says Samira.

Why does it have to be at night? asks Bashir. What sort of work is it that one can only do at night?

Important work. Secret work. Work that no one must know your friend is doing for me. Work that will bring him a very great deal of money. Money with which he can buy fat, wheat, tea and everything else that his family needs to live.

I will be here, says Samira.

How are you going to do that? Bashir asks his friend when they are back up on the mountain.

Man che midanam.

I will come with you.

You are a true friend. Samira sees the fear in Bashir's eyes and says, I'm scared too.

Courage is when you do something even though you are scared.

In the evening, when the stars are in the sky, shine brightly, Samira and Bashir creep from their tents and ride back down into the village.

So, says the disgusting vegetable-seller, after all you didn't come on your own.

We always do everything together, says Bashir. Samir is my friend. I will not leave him on his own.

People are sleeping, be quiet, come in and drink some tea with me. Sit down, you are tired.

We are not tired, says Samira. She takes her Russian gun off her shoulder, squats down, lays it in her lap.

Do you know how to use that? asks the vegetable-seller.

Albatah, says Bashir. He's the best shot I know. He can hit a mountain goat between the eyes from a long way away.

What sort of work am I supposed to be doing? asks Samira.

I want you to take the goods you collected from the butcher today to the next village. My brother lives there. You are to take the parcel to him.

Why must I do that at dead of night?

It's only for your own protection. There is no fighting at night and you can move about unhindered. And also, no one must see where the goods are coming from and where they're going to.

How will I recognise your brother?

He is the owner of the draper's shop.

When Samira and Bashir are about to set off, the disgusting vegetable-seller puts his arm around Bashir's shoulder. Let him go on his own. Why do you want to put your life in danger? Stay here, drink tea with me and tomorrow, when your friend comes back, you can ride back up to your mountain together.

No, says Bashir. I'm going with him. It is a No that leaves no room for the slightest contradiction.

Samira cocks her Kalashnikov, ready to shoot at any moment.

With each step that the horses take, Samira and Bashir

become more and more frightened, Bashir shivers. Samira does not speak any more.

I want to come on your horse with you, says Bashir.

Samira does not look at Bashir, shakes her head, goes on staring straight into the darkness. Even the wind is still. Only the clip, clop of the hooves and the breath of the horses are heard. Nothing else.

The unfamiliar village is bigger than their own. The sandy street is wider, the mud houses are bigger, there are many more stands and stalls. Further on Samira and Bashir even spot a car. When Samira and Bashir arrive at the draper's house, he is still asleep. It is a while before he hears the knocking at the door, opens it, stands in front of the boys, scratches his bottom, yawns, says, has my brother sent you?

Sahihst, says Samira.

The tired draper guides the boys into his shop, takes the goods from them, stows them away under a roll of fabric, calls for tea, and tells them to drink and then sleep.

When Samira opens her eyes again the sun has long risen. The front part of the draper's shop is open. Men, boys, occasionally even a woman, veiled from head to toe, stop and look into the shop. All sorts of sounds and calls come in from the street. In the back part of the shop, which the sun's light does not reach, the tired draper squats along with four other men in the half-darkness on the floor, drinks tea, chats, makes large gestures, listens, shakes his head.

By the large amount of fabric that they wear on their bodies, over their shoulders and on their heads, Samira can tell that these are important men. She cannot hear what they are talking about, but from their expansive gestures and wide eyes she can tell that it is something important.

Samira gets up, stretches carefully so that she does not draw attention to herself, goes over to the men, looks over their shoulders.

One of the men asks, who is the boy?

It's all right, says the draper, that's the messenger.

Maghboul ast, he's handsome, says the man.

There are two of them, says the tired draper. Where's your little friend?

Samira does not speak, nods towards the corner where Bashir is asleep.

Come, boy, sit with us, says one of the men. He grips Samira by the hand, pulls her down to him on the floor. It is unpleasant for her squatting between two strange men, she pulls in her knees, puts her arms around her legs, makes herself small.

One of the men laughs, takes the glittering cap from Samira's head, runs his hand over her long, thick, black hair, says, *maghboul ast*.

Samira twists away, wants to stand up, cannot, remains squatting.

The draper reaches behind him, brings out the parcel that his brother has sent, puts it in the middle on the floor, says, the goods are *maghboul* as well, opens the knot of the parcel and says, *bebin*, look. There are four fat, sticky black lumps wrapped in large leaves. Samira does not really want to speak, she wants to go, she does not want to be part of this circle of men. So she does not know why she opens her mouth and words come out of it. What is that?

Boy, says the man squatting beside Samira, as he slaps her on the thigh and leaves his hand there. This is opium. Best, pure opium.

Samira does not ask what opium is.

You're lucky they didn't catch you. You could have been dead, says one of the men.

The men laugh, chat, slap Samira on the thigh, put their arms around her. You are lucky they didn't catch you, says one of the men and plants a stinking kiss on her cheek.

One of the other men says, let's go to the bazaar and show the boy where real life happens. They take Samira and Bashir between them, go into the busy main street where there are so many people that the sand swirls up under their feet. Men and donkeys carry heavy loads. Men cook food for other men on their carts. Unlike in their own village, there are even women walking around here. Cars, animals, carts and cabs jingle and jangle noisily. Boys sit at the side of the street. In the tea-houses and the entrances to their shops, men sit smoking water-pipes.

At a heavy wooden door the draper and his four friends stop, pay some money, push Samira and Bashir into a narrow room. All the noise and stench make even swallowing difficult. Samira holds her hand in front of her mouth so that the food she has in her belly does not come back out into her mouth. Two men, with more muscles than Samira has ever seen before on a man, are wrestling with each other, half-naked. Samira does not know the reason they are wrestling, the reason why they are doing it in a house and not under God's sky. Samira does not know the reason for the draper and his four friends to have come here, and why they have brought Samira and Bashir with them. Samira knows only that her head is spinning.

All morning Samira and Bashir are pushed back and forth, they drink tea, drink something that looks like water but burns in their throats like poison. They see a man who fights a tired old bear and wins. In a tea-house, they see the first television of their lives. Samira and Bashir eat dal with rice, smoke a water-pipe, see singers and musicians performing a noisy, colourful spectacle. They are men who wear women's clothes, have bright colours on their faces, like brides. The *halkon* dance like women, spin their bodies like women, put their heads on one side like women, put their fingers in their mouths, throw lustful glances at the men, glances that are full of lust, glances with which they arouse the men's lust.

Do you like it? asks one of the men. He puts his arm around Samira and hugs her hard.

Samira shakes him off, says, I don't like men who pretend to be women. And I don't like men who put their arms around other men.

After all their looking at men in women's clothing, and being touched, the men say, we will go to the mosque.

Neither Samira nor Bashir have ever been in a real mosque. Shoulder to shoulder the men are standing in the courtyard outside the big building with the blue dome. With their eyes on the red fireball in the sky, their palms open, ready to receive God's blessing. The men utter their *be-isme-Allah* with great intensity, stand in a row behind other rows, kneel, bow, rise at the same time. The men's voices become one. While the boys and men in the front row bow very low and touch the floor with their foreheads, the draper and his four friends stare at the bottoms of the boys and men in front of them, gesture to one another, licking their lips.

After the prayer the draper and his four friends kiss and hug one another and go back to the draper's house.

Two of the men grab Samira and Bashir by the hands, pull them along behind them, say, time for a rest, and do not even let go of the boys when they resist and refuse to go with them.

Samira is lucky, she is able to break away, runs to Bashir, pulls and tugs at him until he is free too. The men laugh, scratch their bottoms, burp, finally give up running after the boys.

Samira and Bashir run as fast as their legs will carry them, jump on their horses, click their tongues and ride off at a gallop. At the edge of the village they are stopped. Armed men block their path. They say, the enemy is everywhere, and is just waiting for stupid boys like you. If you ride off now, it will be certain death for you. The men send the boys back into the village.

Samira and Bashir ask around, find cheap lodgings where other travellers lie asleep, side by side.

At first Samira keeps her eyes wide open, holds her Russian gun firmly in her hand, hears every snore and every fart, every cock-rub and every groan, until she is too tired. Her sleep is light. She opens her eyes, in the darkness recognises that the man next to Bashir has slid right up to him, has put his arm around him, kisses the nape of his neck and slowly, very slowly starts to rub Bashir's manhood. The man holds Bashir's mouth shut, has wrapped his leg around him so that he cannot move. The man pushes his body back and forth, rubs Bashir's manhood up and down, his groans gets louder and louder. Bashir lies next to Samira, looks into her eyes, knows she sees him, knows his friend will find a way to help him. Samira draws the dagger from her boot, holds it in front of the man's closed eyes, slowly presses it down on him. The man gives a start, jerks his head back, opens his eyes. Samira waits until Bashir has pulled up his *shalvar-kamiz,* walks quietly to the door, she jumps to her feet, creeps over the other sleeping men, jumps down the steps, disappears with her friend into the darkness.

They spend the rest of the night under a cart in the street shivering with fear and cold. When, with first light, people and life return to the streets and alleyways of the scary village, Samira jumps to her feet, swings herself on to her horse, immediately wants to go back to her own village.

Why the hurry? asks Bashir. In a voice that is full of calmness, as though all the things that had happened had not. What can happen now? Yesterday I saw a shop that sold books. We will go there now.

Samira does not know why she follows her friend, but she does.

The owner of the bookshop is sceptical when the two nomad boys come into his shop, but he does not have the heart to throw them out straight away.

Since the outbreak of war, books are no longer being written or printed. Fewer and fewer people can read, and hardly anyone can afford such an expensive luxury. Bread, fat, tea, flour are more important.

Bashir touches the books as though they were glass and liable to break. He touches the pages with two fingers, careful not to open them too wide. He prefers to tilt his head on one side and lean over to glance between the pages rather than break the spine of the books.

Samira prefers to look in the big books, the ones that do not have so many words and are full of pictures instead. Two pictures in particular catch her attention. The first shows a young man who is full of strength. The man holds his bow stretched taut. In the second picture the arrow is flying through the air and the young man is lying on the ground. He is dead.

Samira reads the heading. Arash the archer.

Arash was really an old man, but the poet preferred young men, so he drew him young, the bookseller says.

Samira and Bashir look at one another. We know some men who like young men, too.

Arash is a *pahlevan*, a hero, a warrior, the bookseller continues. He lives in a country where war has raged for many years. One day the king calls Arash to him and says, I have allied myself with the king of our enemies. We are tired, our people are tired. Tired of all the wars, tired of all the killing and of being killed. The king of our enemy and I have agreed to a peace. Who will be the victor? asks Arash. Where will the border between our country and theirs be?

The king looks at Arash says, that, my friend, is in your hands. You are the best and the strongest archer. I have decided that you are to climb the high mountain. You will stretch your bow and fire your arrow. The place where your arrow lands will be the border between our country and our enemy's.

That's how it is to be, says Arash, and climbs on to the highest mountain. All the men, all those who are brave and those who are not so brave, follow him. Arash strips to the waist, turns to the men, speaks to them one last time, says, my body is free of pain and illness, my soul is pure and free of guilt. I will summon all my forces to fire this arrow further than I have ever fired an arrow before. Wherever it lands, that is the place through which the border of our beloved homeland will run. I am old. When I have fired my arrow, I will lose my life with it. I will give my life to my homeland. Arash says that, stretches his bow, fires the arrow and, while it is still airborne, drops lifeless to the ground.

Where does his arrow land? asks Bashir.

In the roots of a young tree that grows far, far away on the bank of a river, says the kindly bookseller.

Samira thinks. She does not know whether or not she likes the story and asks, is the tree still alive, at least?

The kindly bookseller laughs until tears come to his eyes. Laughs. Laughs until Samira and Bashir laugh as well.

A Separation

This tent is no use to us any more, says one-armed grandfather.

It falls to pieces if you only look at it, Samira says and laughs.

Then stop looking at it, says Bashir.

Samira closes her eyes to avoid looking at the poor old felt tent lest it falls apart, taps her way around with her eyes closed and her arms outstretched, runs into Bashir's arms, hugs him, presses him to her for just a little too long and does not know why.

Gol-Sar sees that, stomps, says stupid boys. There is nothing to laugh about.

Samira loves the felt tent. When winter comes, the *kuchi* dismantle their tents and move south from the mountains to escape the snow and the deadly cold, it is like saying farewell to a good old friend whom she has to leave behind.

Four tents have come and gone in Samira's short, full life. Samira was there when they were pummelled, trodden and stamped. Along with the other children, Samira divided up the animal hairs on the sandy floor, rolled about in the wool, watched the men and women beating the thick cloth flat with sticks. The smell of animal hair comes back to Samira, it tickles her skin, feels soft and furry under her feet. The animal hairs snuggle up to one another, weave into a thick mat. Samira shuts her eyes, hears the laughter from Before. It is a laugh that does not know the difference between Samir and Samira. The loveliest child-laughter in the world. Samira sees her mother as she was Before. A mother who had not yet lost all reason. She sits with the other women on the low mud wall over which the felt will be stretched. Her mother sings, raises her child into the sky, stitches brightly coloured strips of fabric around the edge of the felt. Samira wants to stay. Never again wants to open her eyes. Wants to stay there, in order not to lose Before.

Why does Before have to pass away?

Man che midanam.

Samira hears the sound of the stones that the women use to knock the short pegs into the earth, fasten ropes to them, stretch the felt.

Where are all the women from Before?

Man che midanam.

Samira. Poor Samira, who are you talking to? asks the invisible listener. Come back.

Samira, with her eyes closed, lies beneath the tent from Before. Through the sides of the tent the light and the warmth of the sun, the wind, the lambs, the other nomads, the rapists all enter. First into the tent and then into her mother's body. Believe in your amulet, says her mother. It will protect you and destroy everything and everyone that seeks to do you harm. *Shhshh*, do not worry, her father says each night. Be without sorrow. Give all your pain and worry to the wind. Lay everything that makes you miserable on its wings. It will take it away, will bear it out of the tent and free you from it.

Samira opens her eyes, comes back. Back to Samir and her tent of rags.

My father lied, says Samira.

Come on, move yourself, says Daria, knocks the dust out of the felt. First my son was mute, now he talks and talks and does not stop talking. Daria shoos away the fly in front of her face, the fly that is not even there. My son talks and talks and does not notice how stupid the words are he speaks. Daria hisses her words. Like a snake.

Samira obeys, collects the ragged pieces of felt, lays them out in the field, beats the dust from them, swings her stick, draws back her arm, beats at the felt. Screams as she does it. Screams. Screams. Wildly. Full of rage. As though it was not felt that she is beating, but the men who took her mother's honour, who stole her reason. As though the felt was the guilt that defeated her mother. As though the felt was her own father, who was stupid, went to war and allowed himself to be shot.

Hoho, boy. Stop. Stop that, shouts one-armed grandfather.

Samira does not hear him, beats, strikes, screams.

It's my fault, screeches her mother, tears at her hair, scratches her face, gazes at her daughter-son with eyes that have no reason. Bashir throws himself on his friend, pulls him to the ground, sits on his chest, holds his wrists, looks into his eyes that are full of tears.

Samir. My friend. That is all Bashir says.

Samira stops fighting, lets the strength go from her arms and legs. It's all right, she says. Quietly. So that no one hears. Only her friend Bashir.

Come, says Bashir, we will go to the stream.

We will go to the stream, says Samira. Full of longing. For peace, for calm, for Before.

You have become strong, says Samira.

I have, says Bashir. Step by step. Just as you have said.

You have become beautiful, says Samira.

Bashir smiles.

I cannot find a way out any more, says Samira. We have no money, no flour, no tea, we have no donkey, no tent, we have nothing left. All we have are our horses, my gun, some chickens and a few meagre belongings.

Bashir does not say, God is great, he will provide. He says, we will go to the South, find work. We will earn some money and beat felt for a new tent for you.

Bashir, my little friend, my dreamer, says Samira. It is already winter up in the mountains. Everyone is dismantling their tents. Everyone is moving south. Everyone. Except us.

What? Bashir does not understand. Are you not going to move?

Samira shakes her head. One who wants to move needs skins, needs money, needs donkeys, mules and a tent. We have none of that.

We belong together, says Bashir. In all the winters that have come and gone we have gone south together. We will move together this winter as well. We will leave no one behind.

Samira lowers her eyes. My poor friend, come back to the real world. You will leave us behind this winter. It is not your fault. You will have to do it. We have all lost animals in the years of drought, our herds are wretched, no one has the money to drag anyone else through the country and the long winter.

I will talk to my father, says Bashir. He'll help you.

Stop dreaming. Even your father cannot help us. Samira looks into the sky, sees a big silver bird that is not a bird, that is an aeroplane, says, if my mother and my one-armed grandfather were not here, if I were alone, I would move with you, I would find the foreigners, stay with them, I would become a *pilot* and fly away.

Where to?

Anywhere.

Without me?

You are a dreamer, says Samira. She hugs her friend, leaves him sitting by the stream. She goes to her one-armed grandfather, to her mother who has lost her mind, and the scraps of felt that are no longer a tent.

As though the felt is still stretched, her one-armed grandfather sits on the low mud wall. He stares at the bundles and the few belongings, hums to himself, talks to himself, rubs his knee with his one arm which was also injured in the mine, does not notice his grandson coming.

As though the felt were still stretched, Samira walks round the low mud wall, walks in through the place where the entrance was, squats down on the floor in front of her one-armed grandfather, the place where she has always sat, says, now you have lost your home as well.

One-armed grandfather gives a start, comes back to the real world, says, I have lost everything, first my mother, then my father, then my sons, then my arm. But in return I found you. That is how life is, says one-armed grandfather. He wants to go on but cannot because tears are rising into his throat.

Samira smiles, finishes her grandfather's sentence for

him. That is how life is, she says. Life is losing. Life is winning.

Her grandfather nods, says, that's how it is.

Samira lies down on her back, narrows her eyes, spreads her arms, rises up into the blue sky, floats all the way to the huge silver bird.

What are you doing? asks the invisible listener.

Samira does not pay attention to him.

Hey. You. Girl-boy. I am talking to you. Answer my question. What are you doing?

Samira still does not pay attention to him.

Stop pretending to be stupid, says the invisible listener. You are not a child any more.

I know, says Samira.

You have lost your childhood, says the invisible listener.

Samira ignores him, closes her eyes, moves her mouth, speaks words without knowing them, says, summers and winters come and go, they become birds, flock together and fly away.

You have lost it, says the invisible listener.

Samir does not pay attention to him and says, some people do not lose even once in their lives. Nothing. Other people always lose. Everything.

What have you lost? asks one-armed grandfather.

Samira opens her eyes, smiles, says, Nothing. I have won you.

One-armed grandfather strikes his one arm on his leg, wipes a tear from his eye, says, I know. In your short life you have already lost more than many of us old people have. My heart breaks, because in a beautiful country like ours a young and precious life like yours is being wasted. Every day, every hour, valuable young lives are being thrown away.

My life has not been thrown away, says Samira.

Look around you, says her one-armed grandfather. That is all that wars and hunger have left us with. What sort of life is that? What future can anyone build from a life like this?

Any future, says Samira, looks into the sky, nods and says, any future I want.

You are right, says one-armed grandfather. We should not complain. We should thank God for everything he has not taken from us. You go to school and you work hard, you have a keen mind and you are a fighter.

Samira nods, looks into the sky, does not say, my heart is full of stones, full of fear, fear that people might discover that Samira is Samir. That Samira is a liar.

I am frightened, she says.

I know, says her one-armed grandfather. He looks into the sky. The first snow will come today.

Samira says, then let's set off.

Right now?

Right now.

Without saying goodbye to your friend Bashir? asks her one-armed grandfather.

Without saying goodbye to Bashir or anyone else.

It is dark by the time Samira, her mother and her one-armed grandfather reach the valley, they don't go into the village.

Lest we alarm the people, says her one-armed grandfather.

But the people know you and me, says Samira.

We will go into the village when it is light, like proper people, not like thieves creeping about under cover of darkness.

Outside the village Samira leans the long poles of their tent against the remains of a mud wall, lays the pieces of felt upon them, builds a roof, closes off one of the side openings with the bundles and anything else that comes to hand. On the other side of the triangular opening she stacks the baskets of chickens and their other possessions, and tethers their four horses. Samira lays the rest of the felt on the floor, beneath the crooked roof. It is small, but they have enough room to sit, to make a fire, eat and sleep.

Samira sits on the floor, strokes the soft, warm nose of her father's stallion, which pokes through the crooked felt roof. Samira looks into the fire, says, we have a roof over our heads, we have four strong horses, we have eaten.

She smiles, looks at her one-armed grandfather, then at her mother, says, and I have a grandfather who has lost one arm, and I have a mother who sometimes loses all her reason, but I am not alone, and I give thanks to God for that. Samira says that and laughs. Laughs until tears come to her eyes.

You are a good boy, says her mother and runs her hand over her daughter-son's black hair, which is as long and full as the hair of a real young *kuchi* man.

In the morning Samira wakes up first, walks outside into the milky air. Outside is not much colder than it is under the crooked roof. Samira's breath and the breath of the horses turn into little clouds that hang in the air. Everything is silent. Only the snorting of the horses can be heard. Samira pulls on her boots, wraps herself in her *patu*, squats on a big stone, looks up the mountain.

You left without saying goodbye, says the invisible listener.

I did, says Samira. Quietly.

For what reason did you do that?

For what reason do you ask so many questions?

No one forces you to answer my questions.

Samira does not pay attention to the invisible listener.

I know the reason why you left without saying goodbye.

Stop tormenting me.

I'm not the one who is tormenting you. Look at me. I don't even exist. How could I torment you?

Samira plays her flute.

You left without saying goodbye because you did not want to sell your horses to the commander, says the invisible listener.

Go away. Leave me alone, says Samira, goes on playing her flute. Quietly. So that she does not wake her mother and her one-armed grandfather.

Now your friend is gone, says the invisible listener. And his sister is gone, too. They are all gone. I see that you miss them.

I do. I miss them both. I miss Gol-Sar and I miss Bashir.

I see that it hurts.

It does.

You kissed her, says the invisible listener.

I did not.

I was there. I saw it. You nearly kissed her.

What has that got to do with you? asks Samira. She turns her back on the invisible listener.

Hey. Girl-boy. Look at me. Was it Samira who nearly kissed her? Or was it Samir?

Be quiet. Go away, says Samira.

What difference does it make whether I am quiet or not, whether I go or not? I am invisible.

None. No difference at all, says Samira.

Do you like the sister more than the brother?

Samira pretends no one has asked a question, goes on playing her flute.

Your song is full of pain, says the invisible listener.

Samira turns back to face the mountain, picks up stones, throws them in the direction of the invisible listener. She throws them where she thinks his head is.

He does not pay attention to the stones, says, I am waiting. You owe me an answer. You have not yet told me which of the two you like better. The brother or the sister? The invisible listener leans back, narrows his eyes. That is how it is, he says, catches the stones that Samira throws at his head, and throws them behind him. Strictly speaking it is none of my business, but you really should not take pleasure in either the brother or the sister. For you are Samir, a young man, so you may not come too close to Gol-Sar. But we both know that you are Samira, a young woman, so you may not come too close to the brother.

Damn this. I don't want to hear anything more about it. Just clear off, says Samira.

There is going to be a lot of snow, says the invisible listener. It is going to get cold. You have no tent and very little to eat. Do you want to spend the whole winter here under this funny felt roof? You know that will not do. You will perish if you don't find a solution.

We will not, says Samira. None of us will perish.

How are you going to prevent that?

Samira plays her flute.

Hey, Girl-boy. Answer my question. What are you going to do?

The right thing, says Samira. I am going to do the right thing. She wraps herself even more firmly in her *patu*, leaves the invisible listener sitting, climbs down the steep path into the village.

I am looking for a place to spend the winter, says Samira to the kindly teacher, and I need work.

Great God, says the kindly teacher. Boy, where do you think we are? This is the end of the world. The mountains are already full of snow. It won't be long and the winter will come to us and the village as well.

Samira stands there and watches the teacher walking and thinking and pushing his wire spectacles back up his nose. At the end of all that the kindly teacher says, all right then. I will talk to a few people. We will find a solution. The kindly teacher puts his hand on Samira's shoulder. Be without worry.

Fourteen days come and go, the kindly teacher talks to all imaginable people in the village, fourteen days during which Samira tries not to worry, during which it becomes colder and colder, the snow comes closer and closer, more and more water falls from the sky. It rains. Rains so much that Samira cannot get the felt dry any more. The water comes from above, from the sides, from below, from everywhere. Samira carries big stones and small stones to her crooked roof and stacks them around their dwelling. The water finds its way, burrows its way in between the stones, becomes thin, long snakes of water. They creep across the floor, where Samira, her mother and one-armed grandfather sit, eat, sleep. The blankets are wet, the bundles are wet, the wood is wet, the fire is wet, it stinks, smokes, hisses and tries to go out. After fourteen days the snakes of water are still. They no longer weave their way among the blankets, the bundles and the fire. The snakes of water have stiffened, become snakes of ice. The air has a different smell. Outside there is no splashing and rattling. Everything is as still as death. The felt roof is not dripping any more, the drips have turned into icicles, which hang from the felt like daggers. Even the wind is not drifting beneath the crooked roof any more. The icy cold is no longer icy, does not hurt any more. The breathing of the horses, the snores of one-armed grandfather are hollow.

Samira peels herself out of her damp blankets, which are hard and stiff, pulls on her damp boots, wraps herself in her damp *patu*, goes outside. The world is lost. Has disappeared beneath a white blanket. There is snow everywhere. Samira cannot see the mountain any more, or the path up to their plain, the steep path down into the village, the walls and roofs of the village. Nothing. Everything is covered with snow. Snow for as far as Samira can see. Everything is clean. The horses shake the snow from their heads and backs, snort and whinny quietly. Samira looks into the sky, closes her eyes, catches the fat flakes with her tongue, looks around, finds it is beautiful as it is. White and calm. Calm and white.

Samira unties the horses, swings on to the stallion's back, clicks her tongue, pulls the other horses behind her, rides slowly and carefully so that she does not disturb the white, does not shatter the stillness.

Snow times are peace times, the commander had said. When the snow comes, the war goes away.

Samira closes her eyes to feel as though her father is riding along beside her. What is the reason for the war to go away? she asks.

War is scared of snow, her father whispers.

I am scared too, says Samira. She looks around for her father, but does not see him. She rides down the steep path into the village, where the people are still sleeping, rides through the empty alleyways, past the mud huts, the school, the place where the nice dal-seller sets up his stall and his wooden benches in the summer. Samira rides out into the fields, through the deep snow, to the trees. She pushes the snow aside, collects branches and logs, rides back to her crooked felt roof, unloads the wood. Quietly. So that her mother and her one-armed grandfather do not wake up.

But Daria does wake up, sees her daughter-son, closes her eyes, does not move, so that Samira does not know she is awake. Samira stacks the branches and logs beneath the crooked roof so that they support the wet, heavy felt, shoulders her gun, goes back out, leaves the stallion behind, takes the other three horses along, rides back down the steep path to the village.

What are you going to do? asks the invisible listener.

The right thing. I am going to do the right thing, says Samira, and goes to the nice dal-seller.

You are drenched to the bone, he says. Take your boots off, come to the fire and drink some tea.

If I don't get any help now, says Samira, all three of us will be dead soon.

My poor boy, says the nice dal-seller. I have nothing myself. And the truth is that the other villagers are in the same situation. They would not have stayed in the village if they had the money to move to the South.

But someone must help me, says Samira.

There is only one who may be able to, says the nice dal-seller. Quietly. Although there is no one else there who could hear him. It is the disgusting vegetable-seller. He is the only person who has money and who has stayed here anyway. He has too many enemies everywhere else. He stayed because he has so much money that he can buy anything, because he possesses everything a person needs to survive here in the village, even in the harshest winter.

I know what he does, says Samira. I know the reason he is rich.

I know you know, says the nice dal-seller. But I advise you, my boy, do not talk about it. Do you hear? Say nothing. Do not talk to anyone about it. He is dangerous.

Samira has no choice. She goes anyway.

A STABLE

What do you want? asks the disgusting vegetable-seller.

I have a deal for you, says Samira.

The disgusting vegetable-seller scratches his fat belly, laughs, says, you say you have a deal for me? Clear off, fool. It is cold, I want to get back to my warm stove.

I am cold too, says Samira and smiles.

The disgusting vegetable-seller looks at Samira, looks up and down the alley, sees there is no one else nearby, says, all right, come on then, warm yourself up and tell me about this deal of yours.

Samira tethers the horses, follows the disgusting vegetable-seller, takes off her wet boots by the entrance to the room, sits down on the floor beside the roaring stove, takes her gun off her shoulder, puts it in her lap, clutches it tight. With both hands. The disgusting vegetable-seller sits down on the cushions next to Samira. Boy, your clothes are steaming, here, have some tea, he says and drains the dregs of his glass, looks at Samira, shakes his head. You are not looking good.

I'm fine, though, says Samira. She stares at the roaring stove to avoid looking at the disgusting vegetable-seller.

In summer, when you brought the goods to my brother, you were prettier. Are you hungry?

No, Samira lies. At the end of all the lies that Samira tells this morning, the disgusting vegetable-seller leans forward, narrows his eyes, comes so close to Samira that she smells his breath, says, however things may be, my boy, back in the summer I would have paid a lot of money for you, but today I don't like you any more. Look at you, you are as thin as a stick of sugar-candy. Today you are practically worthless.

Samira does not show her fear, her terror. It is not me, says Samira, amazed at her voice, which is calm and relaxed. What would you want from a boy who is as thin as a stick of sugar-candy?

Who is it, then? asks the disgusting vegetable-seller, as he scratches his belly. Then a new idea comes into his head. He raises his eyebrows. Is it your little friend? Even better. He licks his lips, leans back, lays his hand on his cock, holds it, says, I liked him even better than you, my boy, we're in business, name your price.

Samira does not think for long, says, I want a place that is big enough for me, my mother and my grandfather, enough food and wood to get through the winter.

The disgusting vegetable-seller smiles to himself, squeezes his cock, asks, is he worth that much?

Samira looks the disgusting vegetable-seller straight in the eyes, says, it is neither me nor my friend. It is my horses.

The disgusting vegetable-seller takes his hands off his cock immediately. God almighty. You will pay for this impertinence.

Samira does not know where she gets all her courage from, says, I would like to sell you my horses. After all, it cannot do any harm for a man like you, who sends his goods around the whole country, to own a few good and fast horses.

The disgusting vegetable-seller narrows his eyes, says, you think you're really clever, don't you? You think a fool like you can swindle someone like me? Speak, boy. Tell the truth.

You want the truth? I will tell you the truth. The truth is, I don't like you. The truth is, I don't want to sell my horses. The truth is, I will die if you don't help me and take my horses. But it is also true that my horses are worth much more than a place for me, my mother and my grandfather. The horses belonged to my dead father, the famous commander from the upland in the Hindu Kush. My horses are some of the best *buzkashi* horses in the whole of the Hindu Kush. That is the truth. In the summer you can sell the horses for a great deal of money. You have the power to decide.

The disgusting vegetable-seller falls silent, smooths his beard, looks at Samira, thinks and considers, considers and thinks.

Samira looks at the disgusting vegetable-seller, sees that he is filled with pity. A pity that he soon loses again.

The stable that he lets Samira have for the winter is dry, but the mud walls let a lot of cold through. Samira sees straight away that the wood, the wheat, the tea and the other provisions that the disgusting vegetable-seller gives her in return for three of her horses will not be enough to see them through the whole winter. She pleads, begs and scolds, but the disgusting man is ruthless. Either you agree, or the deal is scrapped.

Samira agrees.

You did the right thing, say her mother and her one-armed grandfather.

It takes more than half a day for Samira and her one-armed grandfather to drag their bundles, the baskets of chickens that are barely alive, the scraps of wet felt, the four long wooden poles, the oil lamp and themselves through the deep snow to the stable. At the end of all the carrying and stamping through the deep snow it is dark. Samira and one-armed grandfather are wet. Water is dripping from them.

Daria says, God is great, he has provided in the past, and he will provide now, too.

Yes, God has provided, says Samira, looking down at herself, I am as scrawny as a stick of sugar-candy. Samira laughs. Laughs so as not to cry. Like a wet stick of sugar-candy.

Daria does not show her fear, does not want to see how thin her child is, sees only that Samira has lost her amulet. Daria falls silent.

One-armed grandfather lights the oil lamp, turns the flame down so that it does not use up too much oil, says, who knows whether he even exists?

Who knows whether who exists? asks Samira.

Whether God exists, he says.

Daria rummages and burrows, looks for something, but does not say what it is that she is looking for.

Samira sits by the little fire that her mother has made, stretches out her bare feet, shivers. Her mother puts a blanket around her daughter-son's shoulders. The blanket is damp, provides no warmth. One-armed grandfather puts another piece of wood on the fire. It is too small, the fire does not get any bigger, does not get any warmer. The stallion snorts, whinnies quietly, its breath becomes a little cloud, hangs in the cold air. Daria puts her hand on her child's hot brow. One-armed grandfather puts stones on the

fire, then lays the hot stones under Samira's damp blanket.
The mother lies down next to her daughter-son. Very close
to her so that her own heat may warm her cold child. But
Daria's own body is cold, cannot warm her child's body.

My child is dying, says the mother. It is my fault. It is
because she has lost the *ta-vis*. My poor Samir has
sacrificed himself. And I allowed it to happen.

Your child is tough, says one-armed grandfather. If he
survives this night, he will make it. One-armed grandfather
puts his hand on his grandchild's brow, says, he's on fire. He
is on fire and is freezing at the same time.

Daria fills her pot with snow, melts it, makes the water
boil and simmer. Puts tea in the pot, lifts the head of her
half-dead daughter-son, trickles hot tea into his mouth.
Daria finds her reason, finds the pictures of Before. The
pictures of her daughter-son sitting in the field with his
horse lying down at his feet and putting his head in his lap.
Daria untethers the stallion, says, lie down, give your
warmth to my child.

Leave him be, says one-armed grandfather. You have lost
all reason. Horses never lie on the ground.

Daria knows better.

The stallion obeys, lies down on the floor. Close. Very
close to Samira's cold body. Daria rubs her child's cold feet,
prays to God that she may find the amulet, puts another
piece of wood on the fire, speaks to her child. Stay alive, she
says. Who will protect me if you die?

One-armed grandfather looks into the fire, keeps silent,
weeps. Weeps until the night goes away. When day comes,
he wipes the tears from his eyes, wraps himself in his *patu*,
goes. When he comes back, he brings with him the kindly
teacher. He has a dry blanket, a warm jacket, a dry loaf, a

can of milk, a book, a bottle of green oil. The friendly teacher opens the bottle of oil. Take his shirt off, he says, we will rub his back and his chest with it.

Daria does not take her daughter-son's shirt off, pours oil into her hand, pushes her hand up under Samira's shirt, rubs her chest, her back with it, covers her up with the dry blanket, pours the milk into the pot on the fire, trickles warm milk into her child's mouth. Daria sees the pictures from Before, when she put her milk-filled breast into her child's mouth, tiny Samira suckled on it, her eyes closed.

Samira lies there, her eyes closed. Only the pictures in her head are full of life. They are pictures of Before. Pictures of the wind playing with her hair. She sits in front of her father on his stallion, he holds her very tightly, very securely, dashes along with her until she flies. It is the picture of how her mother ties the amulet around her neck. And the pictures are of Bashir. Many pictures of Bashir and his sister Gol-Sar. The pictures have life.

It is like before, when he was lying under the tree, says the kindly teacher, the boy was lying under the tree in the school, I made my own bed next to him and read for him every night. The boy was asleep, but still he understood that I was reading to him. The stories saved him. Read to him, says the kindly teacher.

He has no life in his body, says one-armed grandfather, what is the point in us reading to him?

Daria knows the teacher is telling the truth, her child hears even if it has no life in its body. The living words from the book restore the life to Samira's half-dead body. Daria looks at the kindly teacher, says, neither I nor my poor father can read.

Then the other boys will have to wait for their lessons,

says the kindly teacher, opens his book, reads. Reads until he can tell from his pupil's face that he hears. Samira frowns, smiles, moves her lips.

Daria kisses her child's forehead, rubs her chest with the oil again, rubs her feet, her arms, sees that her child's hand is still a fist.

The kindly teacher reads the story of the girl and the calf.

That is a beautiful story, says Daria.

It is, says the kindly teacher. God makes human beings, God gives us life. What we make of it is up to each one of us.

Many days come and go before the breath in Samira's chest does not sound like stones and boulders rolling down the mountain. Finally the blankets, bundles and clothes are no longer wet, the stable finally absorbs the warmth of the fire and the stallion; finally, it is no longer so cold in the stable that the breath from Samira's mouth becomes a cloud and lingers in the air. Samira sits up, looks around, smiles, leans her back which is painful against the wall, asks her mother for a thread from her dress, opens her fist, pulls the thread through her *ta-vis* and ties it around her neck.

I thought you had lost it, says Daria.

I won't lose it. It will stay with me as long as I need it, Samira replies. Many more days and nights must come and go before Samira is not as thin as a candy cane. Many more days and nights must come and go before she can go back to class. Most of the other boys have moved to the warm south with their families. Only a few have stayed. In the summer Samira did not like sitting crammed so tightly next to all the other boys in the stuffy little room. But now, when only a few boys come to class and it is icy outside and fresh snow falls from the sky each day, now that the little stove in the middle of the room roars and makes it warm, Samira likes to sit in the room and learn what there is to learn. Until today, class was a summer word, says Samira and smiles. Since this winter class has become a winter word.

Samira reads, writes, repeats words and sentences, asks a thousand and one questions. She hears stories about people who are free and can say what they want. The kindly teacher says there are places where women are just as valuable as men, where no shame falls upon a man if his children are not sons. The kindly teacher says there are places where men are punished if they hit children, if they beat women.

What is happiness? asks Samira. What is hatred? What is contentment? What is love? Where is God? Where is the devil? Samira asks, what is a pilot?

Samira likes the winter.

Whenever she can, she rides through the deep snow. If I do not keep the horse moving, says Samira, it will become weak. It will fall ill, it will die. Come with me, says Samira to her mother. It is not good for you to spend all day and all night sitting here in the stable. I am afraid you're going to lose all reason again.

People will talk about me, says Daria. They will say, what kind of woman is that, strolling about the place as though she had no home? People will say, Daria is a bad woman.

Samira shrugs her shoulders. You have no home. What do we care about people and their gossip?

The stable is my home. A home that was given to us. People are important for us, says Daria. You go to the people's school. We eat the people's bread. The people do not like it if your mother has no honour.

There are no people around, says Samira. No one is going to see you.

There is always someone around. Leave me alone. It is better this way. Daria speaks quietly, opens her eyes wide. Men came, threw themselves on me. Daria stares at her daughter-son with crazed eyes. I am a woman, my honour must be protected.

Samira leaves her mother alone.

Then you come with me, she says to her one-armed grandfather.

The old man spends all day sitting and lying by the fire, dozing, draws in his legs, stretches them out, lies first on one side and then the other. Look at me. Do you want to kill me? One-armed grandfather laughs. It is a laugh with which he wants to take away his grandchild's worries. A laugh that he quickly loses. I am old and sick, I have no strength. It is cold, my clothes have been thin from the beginning, but now they are worn out, I will die if I go out.

You will not die, says Samira. I will protect you.

Everyone must die, says her one-armed grandfather.

A few days later Samira comes into the stable with a bundle. She has begged the people for clothing for her one-armed grandfather.

The people are good, says Daria. They are good as long as we give them no reason not to be good. It is good if I do not leave the stable and give the people no reason to think ill of us. To think that Samir's mother is a bad woman.

Maybe that is so, says Samira, looking at her one-armed grandfather's empty sleeve hanging down uselessly, says, I will cut it off for you.

Just leave it, says one-armed grandfather. If we cut off

the fabric your arm will get cold if you ever find yourself wearing my warm clothes.

I got them for you, says Samira. I am not going to wear them.

Come here, my boy, says one-armed grandfather. He takes his grandson in his arm, look at you. It would have been good for you if you had brought back some new clothes for yourself as well. Your *shalvar* is so short that I can see your ankles, the sleeves of your *kamiz* are so worn that I can see your elbows.

Samira and her one-armed grandfather stand there like that for a long time and don't say a word. After all that standing and all that silence, one-armed grandfather says, you are bigger and stronger than I am. And you have one arm and one hand more than I have. You are a real man.

Samira enjoys her grandfather's one-armed hug. It feels like a hug with four arms.

Never let anyone or anything hold you back. Walk with your head held high. Never think that a task, a path, a decision is too big for you. However long your journey may be, if you think it is the right one, take it.

Samira wonders why one-armed grandfather is saying so many important things.

And now, my boy, now that I have new clothes, let us visit the nice dal-seller and eat as much dal and rice as our hungry bellies will hold.

We have no money, says Samira.

He will give it to us.

The nice dal-seller is pleased to see Samira and one-armed grandfather. The three of them sit on the floor by the stove, which roars cosily away and gives them its warmth, drink tea that tastes of real tea, talk about everything and nothing, laugh, talk of better times.

Until now dal was a summer word, says Samira, now it is a winter word as well.

One-armed grandfather laughs, and says, just see how clever my grandson is. He will not stay in this little village until he is old, like you and me, he will go out into the big wide world and make his way in life. Nothing and no one will hold him back.

The nice dal-seller looks at his old, one-armed friend, wants to smile and cannot. Who knows, says one-armed grandfather, one day you might be standing by your cart, cooking dal, and looking into the sky and one of those big silver birds will fly over our village. Who knows, it might be my grandson sitting in one of those birds and flying over our village and your dal-cart.

I will point to the sky and say, look. That's Samir, the grandson of my honourable friend, Mahfouz the barber, the man to whom I owe so much. The man I fought alongside with in the war.

One-armed grandfather looks at the nice dal-seller. You are a good and true friend to me. And I have one wish. I ask you to be just as good a friend to my grandson. And just as you have never refused me your help, I hope you will not refuse your help to him either.

One-armed grandfather laughs, and do not forget, my friend, look into the sky when the silver bird comes.

Samira, one-armed grandfather and the nice dal-seller are still laughing when one-armed grandfather puts his arm around Samira, presses her to his heart and holds her there. Very close. Very tight. Then, he is not laughing any more. His arm slips, his head falls into Samira's lap, lies there.

Like a child. Like Samira, who laid her head in her mother's lap. Before, when her father was buried beneath the hill of earth. Samira laughs, runs her hand over the white hair of her one-armed grandfather, looks at the nice dal-seller. Sees that he does not laugh.

One-armed grandfather does not move any more. Never again. Before, Samira's father died. Now it is Daria's father who has died.

He knew he was going to die, says Daria. He knew it was his last day. He went outside so he would not die with us in the stable. He brought you to the nice dal-seller to remind his friend of his responsibility. He went to the nice dal-seller to die because he wanted him to take care of the shroud, the mullah and the funeral.

He went to the dal-seller to eat as much dal and rice as he could to fill his stomach says Samira.

Daria looks at her daughter-son, runs her finger over the scar above her eye. A scab has formed around your heart.

Samira smiles. A smile that turns to tears.

The days and nights come and go. Every morning Samira wakes up, sees her grandfather's empty place beside her, does not hear his breath any more, still feels his arm on her shoulder, does not hear his heart any more. All pictures, all memories whirl and blur, become a sticky, foul-smelling lump.

At first only a pain-snake enters Samira's belly, then comes the fear-snake, then the grief-snake and finally a fourth snake as well. Samira does not know the last one. The snake twists up and down inside her body. It leaves her no room to think, to breathe. Samira does not go to class, lies where she is, sleeps, wakes, bends double with pain, gives a start because she hears the voice of her one-armed grandfather, the voice of her commander father, the voices of Bashir and Gol-Sar. Samira listens. It is still. Only the stallion, her mother and her fire are in the stable. One-armed grandfather is not there. Bashir is not there.

Samira drags her body, which is full of pain, full of snakes, outside the stable. Everything is still. Everything is dark. She squats down in the cold snow and looks into the sky. The cold is good, it eases the pain, calms the four snakes in her belly. Samira leans her head against the mud wall, allows the cold to climb in her body, to rise into her bones. Only when the pain ceases to bite, when the four snakes stop creeping, when her body is stiff and wet, does Samira go back to the stable. Then she sees that where she was squatting the snow has turned red. Red as blood. Blood-red snow. It is Samira's blood. Samira knows the fourth, strange snake is the snake of blood and the blood in the snow is her fault.

Yet another misfortune, says Daria. The amulet has not protected you. The blood makes you a woman. When your father died, your voice came. Now that your grandfather is dead, your blood comes.

Why must I bleed to become a woman? Why must I become a woman at all? What must happen for me to become a real man? Why is that God's will? Why can I not just be the person I want to be? Samira squats in front of her mother, has a thousand and one questions. Daria talks and talks. Gives a thousand and one answers. But Samira does not get the answer she needs. Not at all.

Samira kisses her mother on the forehead, pulls on her boots, puts her gun over her shoulder, leaves the stable, jumps on to her horse, rides out of the village. The snow is deep, Samira makes slow progress. By the stream that is covered in ice she squats down, looks the moon in its bright, cold face, knows her mother is telling the truth, it would mean death for her if she showed her true face. Samira squats in the snow, plays her flute and only returns to the village when the sun casts its first light over the mountain.

Samira unpacks her father's bundle.

Daria saw it. The day the commander went under the hill of earth, Samira went to the stream, stayed there for a long time. Daria followed her, saw her naked daughter lie down in the stream and talk to the water. When she came back from the stream, she had a bundle under her arm. Daria knew the day would come when Samira would tell her what was in it.

Four knots Samira tied. One for herself, one for her mother, one for the commander, one for the children her mother did not pull from her body. Through all the summers and winters that have come and gone, neither Samira nor her mother nor her one-armed grandfather have ever opened the knots. Samira pulls and tugs at the knots, cannot open them, shoves the sickle under the knots, pulls, cuts and tugs until the bundle is open. In it are the boots of her dead commander father, his dagger, his little *buzkashi* whip and a dress. A dress as beautiful as a field full of flowers, made of thick, solid, warm fabric.

My father said the day would come when I would know what to do with these things. I would know which ones I would need for myself. He said that would be the day I make my decision. That day has come, says Samira.

I know, says Daria.

Samira pulls on her father's boots, sticks the dagger into her belt, shoves the whip into her boot, gives her mother the brightly coloured flower-patterned dress. I don't need this, she said. You wear it.

Samira in her father's boots and Daria in her daughter's dress squat by the fire, watch the rags of Daria's old dress being eaten by the flames.

Let it burn, says Samira.

Your father lives on in this fabric, says Daria. His touch, his fragrances and his breath live in it.

Let it burn.

I wiped his blood away with this dress. The weight of his and your heads are in this dress. I carried the bread in my dress when I brought it to him in the field. His love lived between the threads. I dried your tears and his tears with it. Wiped your wounds and his with it. You lay between the great folds of my dress when you were ill.

It is burning, says Samira, and with it burn all sins, all guilt. Let it burn.

I was still a little girl when I wove the red fabric with my own hands, says Daria. The clack, clack of the loom is in my ears. Each time I pulled through the little piece of wood with the bright threads, I prayed to God to send me a man who was decent. A man who would honour and respect me.

Did he do that? asks Samira.

It took a whole summer until the fabric was finally ready, says Daria.

Did your husband respect you? asks Samira.

I washed the fabric in the stream. The fabric lost its blood, dyed the water blood-red. The other girls held their hands before their mouths and giggled and sang. Soon our beautiful Daria with the almond eyes will become a woman. Her blood is flowing into the stream, and it will find its way to the man who will pick up its trail and find Daria and her brightly coloured wedding-fabric and marry her.

Let it burn, says Samira.

I sewed the fabric into a dress, embroidered it with a thousand and one mirrors and pearls. Pieces of mirror to protect me against the evil eye, says Daria.

Did my father protect you? asks Samira.

As I set the mirrors into the fabric, I saw my own face. A thousand and one times. I saw my hope, my future. With every pearl that I sewed on my dress, I expressed a wish and asked God to hear it.

Did he hear your wishes? asks Samira.

I wore this dress when your father married me, when he made me a woman, when he made me a mother, when he made me a widow.

Let it burn.

Everything burns, says Daria. The good and the bad.

Leave it, says Samira.

My new dress is brightly coloured, says Daria. There is nothing of him in my new dress. Neither his tears nor his pain, neither his words nor his love. Neither my desires nor my pleas.

Nor the guilt he placed upon you, says Samira. Let it burn, give it to the fire.

I am letting it burn, says Daria. All that and much more.

AN ENGAGEMENT

Since winter has gone again and Samira and her mother have returned to the upland, Samira squats on her rock every day and waits for her friend Bashir and his sister Gol-Sar to come back to the plain, to come back to her.

Samira is full of happiness because she herself and her mother survived the hard winter. She is without happiness because her one-armed grandfather has died. She is full of happiness because he was laughing when he died. She is without happiness because her mother spent the whole winter locked up in the stable and has lost even more of her reason. She is full of happiness because she has been to class and learned a great deal that is new and important. On the other hand she now knows there is so much that she will never be able to know because the rest of the world, with all its knowledge and wealth, is so far from her village, the mountains and her upland in the Hindu Kush. Samira's heart still suffers pangs because she had to give away her Azad and the two other horses to get through the winter. She is full of happiness because she was able to keep her father's stallion. Samira is without happiness because the blood that makes her a woman has come, she is full of happiness because it has come and she has finally decided to wear her father's boots and be a man. A real man. So the winter has gone and Samira is half full of happiness and half without happiness.

Since she has been back in her upland, Samira has been getting more and more accustomed to go hunting, to kill animals and spill their blood. In the beginning she and her mother eat most of the meat caught. Samira brings the rest down into the village and gives it away. To the kindly teacher and the nice dal-seller, the families of the other boys from class, even to the disgusting vegetable-seller.

The butcher proposes a deal to Samira. She sells him the shot game and earns enough money to buy necessities for herself and her mother. Fat, tea, wheat, even a tent. It is not a big tent and not new, but there is enough room in it for her mother and herself.

Samira sits on her rock, plays her flute, looks towards the path. She just thinks, perhaps the other *kuchi* will not be coming back, perhaps the damned war has eaten them up, perhaps they and their animals perished miserably in the drought, when at last she hears the sound of men shouting and dogs barking. Finally Samira hears the snorting of horses, the clopping of their hooves, she sees the dust they swirl up, the birds in the sky that herald and accompany the return of the *kuchi*. Finally, they are back.

Samira jumps from the rock, swings on to the back of her stallion, rides towards the other nomads. Even from a long way off she recognises Commander Rashid's family, in the middle of them the yellow scarf and wide, bright skirts of Gol-Sar. She has grown taller and slimmer, moves in a way that Samira does not recognise. Gol-Sar no longer runs and dashes about as she did before the winter, she sways her hips, moves her arms with calm, big gestures, not like a girl, like a woman. A real woman. Samira knows, just as it has come to her, the woman-blood has come to Gol-Sar. Even from a distance Samira can see that the commander has lost half of his sheep, goats, camels, donkeys and mules and his straight, proud back. Samira sees all that and much more. There is only one thing she does not see. Her friend Bashir.

The whole country is dry, says Gol-Sar. Look at our animals, they are thin and weak. We have lost many of them. We need money. The foreigners pay well when you fight for them. Bashir has stayed, he is fighting for them.

Samira does not want to believe what she hears, wants to ride to the South, to look for her friend, bring him back to his homeland, his upland, to her.

Bashir is fighting? In what war? What does it matter to Bashir if the foreigners are fighting the Taliban? It is not Bashir's war. Does Bashir speak the foreigners' language? What kind of foreigners are they? Where do they come from? Why do they fight the Taliban? Bashir and I do not need the foreigners' money, we can earn enough here. We can sell opium for the disgusting vegetable-seller. We can hunt, and sell the meat and the hides. We can catch fish and sell them in the village.

Gol-Sar does not smile, her eyes are lifeless when she says, however all that may be, you can see, your friend is not there.

Samira helps Commander Rashid to erect his tents, to look after the horses. She goes hunting, gives him meat, goes to the stream, comes back with fresh fish, the days come and go but the longing in Samira's heart does not go.

She misses her friend, misses hearing his voice, lying on the rock with him, going into the mountains, sitting by the stream.

God is merciful, says Commander Rashid. Until Bashir comes back, you will replace my son.

I will ride to the South, says Samira, and bring him back. There is enough work here, enough money. Enough of everything.

Not for all the people I have to feed, says Commander Rashid. Do not be foolish, boy. Even if you were to make it to the South, you would never find him. The South is immeasurably big. There are thousands of foreigners there. They shoot anyone they don't know. They have big, heavy weapons with which they can hit the enemy from a long way away, weapons that can reach all the way from here down into the valley. They have aeroplanes from which they drop bombs and missiles.

He'll come back, says Gol-Sar. She looks into Samira's eyes, puts her hand on Samira's arm, sees her father's gaze, snatches her hand away again, lowers her eyes, says, he will come. I know it. Be patient.

Off you go, girl. The commander puts his hands on his hips. Go to the stream, fetch water and make us some tea. I have something to discuss with Samir.

Gol-Sar obeys, takes the pot, goes to the stream, squats down, her feet play with the water and the stones in the bed of the stream, she smiles and is full of happiness. She knows what her father has to discuss with Samir. All through the long winter she talked about it with her brother. She confided in him and told him what was going on in her heart. She begged her brother to talk to their father. All winter Bashir listened to his sister, scolded her, told her to be a decent girl, to have patience, comforted her. Bashir looked at his sister and knew it was too late. His sister had lost her heart. To his own friend. To Samir.

Commander Rashid says, you have been a good friend to my son. He has learned a lot from you. It was only through you that he became a real boy and finally a real man. My son respects and reveres you. It would be no exaggeration if I say that he loves you more than one can love a friend. Bashir loves you like a brother. Friendship between men is sacred. Nothing and no one can replace it. A friend is the greatest protection that a man can have. You are a brother that he has chosen for himself.

Samira plays with her horse's bridle, looks at the commander, does not look at him, gazes into the distance, looks into his eyes, hears his words, understands them, does not understand them, says, if you have a good friend you need no one else in your life.

Commander Rashid strokes his beard smooth, laughs, says, on that you are wrong. Because however close you may be to your friend, every man needs a woman to bear him sons. Bashir's father laughs. Some men even need more than one wife.

Samira does not know where to look, sees Gol-Sar coming back from the stream, she holds the pot in front of her belly, sways her skirts. She smiles, goes into the tent, comes back out, puts the pot on the fire, does not come over to Samira and her father, stays sitting by the fire, glances across at Samira and Commander Rashid, and does not stop smiling.

The commander sees Samira's expression, says, time is a devil. It comes and goes so fast that one has to hurry to be aware of what is going on around you. The commander smiles. When you came to us in the upland, you were so small, he says, indicating with his hand how small Samira was.

Samira does not understand what all this talk is about.

Bashir and my daughter were not much bigger. You spent a lot of time together. No one decent and devout could have reproached me for it. But now you are no longer a little boy, and Gol-Sar is not a little girl. It is not proper and God does not like to see it when a young woman is alone with a young man. God preserve us from that. People will talk, they could think I have no honour.

Samira looks at Gol-Sar, looks at the commander, asks, does that mean I am not to see her any more? No, my boy. Do not worry, says the commander.

I am not worried, says Samira. If you do not want it, I will stay away from your daughter in the future. Your honour and her honour are also my honour.

The commander smiles, says, you are like my own flesh and blood, and you have my complete trust.

Samira does not know why Commander Rashid is saying so many important things.

I know you have no wealth, says the commander. But I also know you are hard-working, honest and sincere. I know you are a fighter and will achieve what you want.

What Samira really wants is to get to her feet and run away.

I know you are alone in this world and you have no one to speak for you. The commander pulls himself up, strokes his smooth beard even smoother, smiles, says, I would like to give you permission to marry my child.

What am I to do? asks Samira, and becomes aware that all the blood is rushing from her body to her head.

Commander Rashid does not laugh, he says, first you will be engaged until you have found a proper job, can buy a proper tent for yourself and your bride. A part of the money you will earn working for me. I want you to prepare my horses for the game.

Samira nods and nods, and does not know why she is nodding.

I am going to get married, says Samira to her mother.

You are going to do what? asks Daria. She looks at her daughter-son. You have lost your reason.

Commander Rashid has said very clearly he wants me to marry Gol-Sar. Samira looks at her mother and laughs. At first it is a quiet laughter, then it gets louder and louder, she loses all reason and her laughter turns turns to weeping.

Maybe we should flee and find somewhere else to go, says Samira.

Maybe we should do that.

Maybe I should just get married.

Maybe you should do that.

Maybe I should go on to my rock and ask God to give me an answer.

Ask your amulet to help you, says Daria.

Samira packs the fresh, warm loaf that her mother has just pulled out of the oven, swings on to the back of her stallion, gallops off. She urges her stallion on until it snorts loudly, its long mane blows in the wind like a flag, its hooves thunder as though trying to ram their way into the earth, none of its four legs touch the ground. The tents of the other nomads, their animals, the nomad children, bushes, rocks, the stream all blur together. The world is a brightly coloured mixture of colours and the thundering of hooves, the snorting of the stallion, Samira's breath. She flies past the cries of the men and boys. *Salam, Samir. Zende bashi. Koja miri?* Greetings, Samir. Long may you live. Where are you going?

Samira does not reply, she does not want people to see how frightened she is. She bends low over her stallion's neck, claws her fingers into its mane. Samira and her stallion cleave together, become one. Half human, half animal.

For the rest of the day and half of the night Samira lies on her rock and thinks and thinks and does not find an answer to the question of what she must do. When Samira hears footsteps in the darkness, she does not need to ask who they belong to. What are you doing here?

I want to visit you, says Gol-Sar.

You father will shoot us.

We are engaged.

But we are not married yet. I am forbidden to see you without a *mahram*. I am forbidden to be alone with you. Forbidden. Do you understand?

Do you not want to be engaged to me?

Samira shrugs. I am not as you think I am.

I know how you are.

Samira looks Gol-Sar straight in the eyes. No one knows who I really am.

Gol-Sar stands at the foot of the rock, holds out her hand, says, help me. I do not care who you really are. I see you as I see you. She lowers her eyes, says, and I like the way I see you.

You don't know what you are saying, says Samira.

Just because I am a girl it does not mean that I don't know what I am saying, says Gol-Sar. And I know I will not find a better man than you. She looks at Samira, lowers her eyes

Samira and Samir   229

in shame, says, besides you are more handsome than anyone else I know.

You will be disappointed, says Samira. I beg you, go to your father and tell him you don't want me. Samira grabs Gol-Sar by the shoulders. You will make us all, your brother, your father, my mother and everyone else unhappy.

Listen carefully and don't say anything, says Gol-Sar. Do you think that if I go to my father and say I don't want Samir, do you think he will say, fine, in that case let us dissolve the engagement?

Will he not? asks Samira, and answers her own question. No. He will not.

The two of them talk and talk, move apart, move closer together, until they are both so tired that they go to sleep. Neither of them notices how close together they have moved, Gol-Sar does not notice that she has put her head on Samira's chest and laid her leg on Samira's belly. Samira does not notice that she puts her arm around Gol-Sar and pulls her tight to her. The girl-man lays his hand on the girl-woman's thigh. The girl-man and the girl-woman hold each other tight. Very tight.

Samira dreams of angels lifting her into the air, above all the mountains and water. She dreams of places and countries she does not know. Of an enormous bird with a head like her stallion, taking her between its wings and carrying her into the sky. Past the stars and the sun to where even God is not. Where the beginning and the end of all things is. Where Nothing is.

Gol-Sar dreams of a beautiful tent that smells of rose-water. She dreams of bowls of clear water, brightly coloured cushions and jewellery that she hangs from the wall of her tent. Gol-Sar dreams of her husband, who laughs, squats next to her, reads the same book as she does, goes into the village with her. Gol-Sar dreams of a man who allows her to not cover her face even in the valley.

At the end of these dreams the girl-man and the girl-woman let go of one another, turn on their sides, turn their backs to each other. They lie there like that for the rest of the night. Back to back.

Only when the sun casts its first light and its first warmth over the peak of the mountain does Samira open her eyes, turns round, shakes Gol-Sar. Gol-Sar jumps from the rock without a glance at Samira, runs down the mountain, climbs on to her donkey, and hurries to get back to her father's tent.

Samira raises her head, watches after Gol-Sar for a moment, stretches herself, yawns, lies down again, sleeps.

Even from a distance Gol-Sar can see the smoke of the fire rising from the tent. She creeps up to it, reaches under the tent-wall, pulls out the clay jug, goes to the stream, splashes water in her face, returns to the tent. Her little sister is squatting outside, chewing on a stone. She sees Gol-Sar, stretches her arms out. Gol-Sar smiles, puts down the water-jug, wipes her damp face with the corner of her dress, picks her sister up, kisses her, lifts her into the air.

Where are you? her mother calls. I need the water.

Gol-Sar smiles, goes into the tent with the jug, looks at her mother, knows she has no idea that she did not spend the night in the tent.

The days come and go, grow warmer and warmer. Samira misses Bashir. Gol-Sar visits Samira on her rock. Samira goes to school. Gol-Sar squats somewhere among the rocks or by the stream, reads and writes and practises and practises. Gol-Sar visits the little girl-woman Firouza.

Firouza tells Gol-Sar that she is sad because she has not yet been able to give the *Hadji* a son. Gol-Sar explains to Firouza that her woman-blood must come before she can have a child. Samira rides past the tent of the former girl prostitute, dismounts, tightens her saddle although it does not need to be tightened, sees the former girl prostitute again has another newborn baby hanging from her breast, last summer's baby is lying in her lap. The former girl prostitute has grown thinner, looks like a stick of sugar-candy. She has a wound above her eye, exactly where Samira has her wound. The former girl prostitute sees Samira, does not smile, just looks at her without really seeing her. Samira rides into the mountains, shoots a goat, brings it to Daria. They pull off the animal's hide, leave it to dry in the sun, cut the meat into pieces, sell most of it to the other *kuchi*. Daria cooks the rest. She brings some of the cooked meat to the former girl prostitute, feeds her, takes her newborn child, washes it.

Samira sells hides down in the village, buys a fresh melon for her mother, drops in on the nice dal-seller, and eats as much dal and rice as her belly will hold. When she pays, the nice dal-seller points into the sky, asks, when will you fly?

Before she goes back to her upland, the butcher orders a whole goat from Samira and pays in advance. Samira buys a length of fabric for her mother, one for the former girl prostitute, a comb and a bottle of rosewater for Gol-Sar, leather and pearls for a new bridle for her stallion.

Every Friday, the day of the *buzkashi* game, Samira collects Commander Rashid's horses, dashes across the plain with them until their muscles are soft and warm. She rubs down the animals and takes them to the playing-field, where Commander Rashid is already waiting. The men say that since Samir has been riding in the commander's horses, the commander has become an even more successful player. The women say the commander's daughter is lucky because she is getting such a good and capable man.

Because the people talk so much about Samir, Daria is constantly checking to see that the amulet is still there, and sews yet more mirrors on to her daughter-son's cap and waistcoat, so that the evil eye does not reach Samira.

After the game Samira and Commander Rashid ride to his tent, squat on the brightly coloured carpet that his wife and daughters have woven. Gol-Sar and her sisters bring the men rice and meat. The little children from the surrounding tents come and join them, eat with them, look at Samira and talk behind their hands. He can shoot a goat from the back of his horse, they say, and he climbs around among the rocks like a mountain goat. The children say, hey, Samir, show us how strong you are.

Samira picks up a girl in one hand and a boy in the other, spins round and round with them, stretches out her arms and spins until the girl and the boy are flying and shrieking. Samira sets the children down, they laugh and laugh because meadow and mountains, people and tents are whirling around them. They shout Samir, Samir, you are the strongest man the Hindu Kush has ever seen.

Samira smiles, says, it is not a question of strength.

What is it, then? cry the children.

It is a question of practise, says Samira.

Samira has told them the story many times before, they know it off by heart, but nonetheless they cry, tell us about the girl and the cow. The children sit around Samira, climb up her back, lay their heads in her lap, ask, and what is the moral of the story? Samira keeps silent, shrugs her shoulders. The children laugh, all shout at once, say, the moral is that if someone wants something he must practise and practise, then he will be able to do it in the end.

The days and nights become birds, flock together and fly away. Samira rides into the mountains, climbs up to the peak, spreads her arms and legs, stands before the rising sun, stands in the middle of the burning red ball, casts a shadow, waits until the sun rises, until she carries the glowing ball. Daria pulls fishes out of the stream, pulls milk out of the teats of the goat, pulls bread out of the oven in the floor, pulls thorns out of Samira's finger, pulls threads in her brightly coloured dress, threads that are supposed to bring good fortune. Gol-Sar squats outside her tent, weaves a bright band of four hundred threads for her wedding. Commander Rashid rides his horses, bends down low, grabs the calf, wedges it under his thigh, rides round the flag, brings the carcass back to the circle that is *helal*. He has learned from Samira, does not throw it, sets it down. Full of respect, full of reverence. Because blood has been spilt, red as the blood that flows in his own veins. Samira squats on the rock, draws a new thread through her amulet, plays her flute, looks into the sun as it takes away its last light, its last warmth, and disappears behind the mountain. The invisible listener squats next to Samira, looks at her, does not say anything. Leaves her in peace. The happiness-snake comes to Samira, does not creep into her belly, lies next to her on the rock, curls up, sleeps. Gol-Sar does what is forbidden, takes off her head-scarf, loosens her plaits, climbs on to the rock, lies down next to her Samir, pushes her body very close to his. In her sleep, Samira senses the familiar body, pulls Gol-Sar to her, hugs her, buries her face in her thick hair that smells of rosewater. Samira smiles in her sleep. Before the sun comes over the mountain with its first light and first warmth, Gol-Sar wakes up, jumps from the rock, climbs on to her donkey, rides to her tent, to her mother who once again does not know that her daughter did not spend the night in her tent.

After nights like that, Samira can neither look her mother nor Commander Rashid in the eye. Samira lies where she is, looks into the sky, sees Gol-Sar's face in the bright stars, with her delicate skin, her almond eyes, her hair that gleams like silk, that is black as night. Samira sees the face of her beloved Gol-Sar and next to it the face of Bashir. Her beloved friend Bashir. Bashir, whom she misses as though someone has torn out a piece of her heart. She lies there like that, sees the two faces in front of her and does not know who it is that sees the two of them. Is it Samira? Or is it Samir?

A REVELATION

My lovely, bright daughter, my brave girl, my beloved Samira, says Daria.

Samira smiles. It is years since her mother has called her daughter. Since her mother called her girl. More years than Samira can remember. So long that Samira has the feeling that her mother is not speaking to her, that she is speaking to another person. To a stranger. Someone she ceased to be a long time ago.

Samira no longer exists, says Samira, smiles, wraps the strip of fabric around her breasts so that no one will see the curves of her womanly body.

You are a beautiful woman, says her mother. A woman who lives the life of men more successfully than any man I have ever known. Daria smiles, looks into the distance as though the men she is speaking about were standing there. More successfully than your own father, says her mother.

Samira smiles and pulls on her white *kamiz*.

Daria looks at her daughter-son, says, had I pulled you out of my own body as Samir, you would not have known life from its harsh side. You have learned to fight, you have learned to take life as it comes. You have learned not to see the loss but the benefit.

Samira combs back her thick, black hair, pulls her colourfully embroidered, glittering waistcoat over her white *kamiz*, says, mother, we live in a country where even the men are not free. Were they free, they would not need to take women's freedom away. One who is free needs not to deny anyone else their freedom.

You say big words, says her mother, catches a bubble so that it does not land in the fire and die with a hiss.

Samira wraps her long scarf round her waist so that no one can see how slim she really is.

Daria sees her child standing in the first morning sun, straight and proud. Tall, with a strong back, with broad shoulders and with her head held high. My bright girl, says Daria. Your strength and sharp mind make you beautiful.

Samira slips her dagger into her scarf, slips her little whip into her father's boot, puts on her glittering cap, touches the amulet around her neck, looks at her mother, goes purpose-fully over to her, bends down to her, runs her hand over her white hair, kisses her on the forehead. Daria shuts her eyes, enjoys her child's strength and her affectionate presence.

Pray for me, says Samira.

That's him, say the men. That's Samir. He is going to be the best *buzkashi* player that the Hindu Kush has ever seen. He is the best rider the Hindu Kush has ever seen, call the little boys, jumping up and down. The girls and women giggle, say, and he is the handsomest man the Hindu Kush has ever seen. May God protect him and preserve him from all evil. May the Lord God grant him a long life, so that we may long gaze upon him.

Samira rides to Commander Rashid's tent, jumps from

her horse before it has come to a stop, bows before the commander. It is only a small bow.

The two ride side by side, as if they are father and son, as if they are king and prince. Samira could go on riding like that for ever, to the end. To the end of her life and the Hindu Kush, to the end of everything and everyone.

When they arrive at the big field where the game is played, the other men cease what they are doing, fall silent, clap their hands.

The musicians tune their instruments. Boys sell water, others sell bread that their mothers and sisters have pulled out of their ovens. Little girls, who are so small that they do not yet have to hide from the eyes of strange men, run around. A few old women, who are so old that they do not have to hide from the eyes of strange men, sit on the hill and wait for the game to begin.

Boy, says the commander. I am going to take the white stallion into the game first. Ride him in.

Samira grips the whip between her teeth, wraps the reins around her wrist, whistles, rides off, urges the horse on. It stamps, its hooves thunder on the ground, as though it wanted to ram them into the earth. It sounds like music, the thunder of the hooves mingles with the snorts of the horse and its jangling bridle.

At the sight of them, the men's hearts are filled with longing. They know they will never be able to ride like this boy.

Samira rides as though she is actually in the game, as though she is being pursued and chased by the other riders and horses. Samira does not know why she does what she does. Further away she sees one of the players who has wedged the calf under his thigh, and wants to ride it round the flag. Samira gives a series of short cries and urges the stallion on until she is riding beside the man with the calf, bends over to him, tugs at the other horse's reins, so that it startles. The rider is not fast enough, Samira pulls the calf away from him, rides around the flag, dashes back to the circle that is *helal*, pulls on the reins, the stallion rears up on its back legs. Samira bends down low, sets down the carcass, bows to the dead animal and the circle.

A shot is fired. The game can begin.

Samira gives a start, wakes from her dream, hurries to bring the commander back his stallion, bows to him, says, forgive me. I was dreaming, I don't know why I did that.

The commander says, that was fine proof of your skill and your strength, but you must be patient, because you are not yet *pochte* for the game.

Samira says nothing, helps Commander Rashid on to the back of his stallion, sits down at the edge of the playing-field, when an arm is laid around her shoulder and a voice whispers in her ear. The arm feels like the arm of her one-armed grandfather.

I have a different opinion. I think you are ready, you are more than *pochte* for the game. It is the nice dal-seller who has sat next to Samira.

Samira is happy that her friend has come to visit, laughs, hugs the old man, asks, what are you doing up here on the upland plain?

I thought I could finally admire you in the game, says the nice dal-seller.

Samira smiles and says, you just did.

That is true. I saw you, and when the time comes for me to go to the next world, I will take your grandfather aside and tell him you are better than any one of these men here.

Samira laughs. It would be nice if you could find my father and tell him, too.

Hey, boy, says the nice dal-seller. And when will the day come when I see the silver bird in the sky and know that is you up there?

Man che midanam, says Samira. Only God knows that. He will tell me when the right time for that and everything else has come.

Boy, look at me, says the nice dal-seller. Look at me closely. My days are counted.

Samira does not smile any more. She sees it. She knows it. She puts her arm around his shoulder, says, you will outlive us all. Just wait. You'll see.

The nice dal-seller shakes his head, laughs and laughs, wipes tears from his eyes, leans his head against Samira's shoulder.

At the end of the game, after listening to music, after the hand-clapping, after all that and everything else the nice dal-seller says that this day has been the finest day he has had in a very long time.

By way of farewell, Samira and the nice dal-seller hug each other, hold each other for a long time. Samira accompanies the old man to the path that leads down into the valley, cannot part from him, walks down into the valley with him, brings him to his hut. It has been dark for a long time, the stars and the moon are shining in the sky when Samira comes back up to her mountain. She knows she will never again see the nice dal-seller.

His God has called him, says the invisible listener.

Samira knows it, climbs up on to her rock, lies down on her back, looks into the sky, feels the weight of the grief-snake on her chest, gives a start because she hears steps that she does not know. Samira cocks her gun, stares into the darkness. No one is to be seen. Everything is silent.

Why do you not weep? says the invisible listener.

Samira pays him no heed, stares straight ahead, sees nothing, hears nothing, says nothing, thinks nothing, becomes nothing herself. A big empty Nothing with a snake on her chest.

Samira closes her eyes, feels the light of the stars, feels the light breeze that settles on her forehead and gently strokes her skin like a finger. A strong, gentle finger that takes the black, empty pictures out of her head. Samira feels the angels who take her by the hands and carry her up, past everything, to where Everything is. To where Nothing has its beginning and its end. Samira spreads her arms out, lets her body drop forward, falls, falls into the arms of her commander. Her father. Samira picks up the stone, places her secret underneath it. Samira climbs back up on to her rock, wants to lie down on her back, pauses, knows she is not alone. Knows someone is squatting behind her. Samira does not move, reaches very slowly for the handle of her dagger, gradually pulls it out, bit by bit, when a hand settles gently on her hand and slips the dagger back in. Samira smiles, lets it happen, does not move, feels the hand on her hand. It is a strong, powerful hand of a man. It is a hand that she is not afraid of. It is as it was before, the hand is like her father's hand. Samira becomes aware of the body sitting behind her. It is the body of a man, a body she is not afraid of. Samira becomes aware of the man's breath. It is a breath without fear. It is as it was before. Before, when she sat on the back of her father's stallion, leant her little body against her father's big, strong body. Samira closes her eyes, like before, leans back, loses her heaviness. Samira loses everything. Loses. Loses, until she realises she is not asleep. Until she realises it is a real body she is leaning against. Without hesitating, Samira draws her dagger, rolls to the side, looks into the face of a man squatting in front of her.

It is a man Samira has never seen before. The man has broad shoulders, his arms are full of power. His hair is long and black, it is full and gleams in the light of the moon like silk. His face is full of grief, full of happiness, full of longing.

Where have you been? asks Samira.

I have been up and down the Hindu Kush, says the man. In all my paths I looked at every stone, searching for the one under which my friend has placed his secret.

Did you find what you were looking for? asks Samira.

I came to hear from you what the secret is I am looking for, says the man.

The two kneel in front of one another, look into one another's eyes in silence.

It is a silence that says more than a thousand and one words.

Slowly, very slowly, Samira lays her dagger down on the rock, stretches out her hand, touches the man's face. The man slowly puts his arm around Samira, draws her to him, hugs her. It is far more than a little hug of greeting. Samira takes the man's face in her hands, looks into his eyes, kisses him on the forehead. The man looks into Samira's eyes, kisses her on the mouth. Samira does not resist.

Samira tells the man that she is betrothed. That her fiancée's name is Gol-Sar. The man knows. Samira tells him that she is going to marry. The man knows. The man tells her that he has seen war, that he has killed the enemy, that not a day has passed when he has not thought of his friend. His friend Samir. Samira knows. The man says he has come back for only one reason. Samira knows. He has come to see his friend. Samira tells him how great her longing has been. For only a single person. For her friend. For Bashir. Bashir knows.

You are behaving like a pair of lovers, says the invisible listener.

Samira does not pay attention to him, lies down beside Bashir on the rock, looks into the sky, says, at long last the stars have regained their brilliance. Bashir rests his head on his hand, looks into Samira's eyes, wants to kiss her forehead, kisses her mouth. Samira lets it happen. First once, then one more time and many times.

You have become a man, says Samira. A real man.

You are beautiful, says Bashir. More beautiful than I remember. You are the most beautiful man I have ever seen.

Samira reflects, thinks, wants to say something, stops reflecting, does not think, says nothing and lets it happen. Bashir draws up his knee, lays his leg on her belly, presses his male desire against her belly. It is like before. Before, Gol-Sar drew up her knee, laid her leg on Samira's belly. Blood rushes to Samira's head, rushes to her belly. Samira does not know which desire is greater. That for Gol-Sar or that for Bashir. Samira likes this one and the other one. Samira lets it happen.

Bashir enjoys his friend's pleasure, holds her from behind.

Samira lets it happen, does not know what is happening, does not know why she is spreading her thighs, does not know why Bashir is doing what he is doing. Samira does not know that she is being turned from a girl to a woman, just knows it feels good.

She feels her body as she has never felt it before, she sinks into Bashir's arms, drowns in his caresses, in his pleasure. Bashir sees nothing. Hears nothing, immerses himself in a world that he does not know. Bashir vanishes, loses his reason.

You think Bashir knows your secret, says the invisible listener. Poor Samira, you are wrong. He knows no more than he did before.

Samira does not pay attention to him, claws her fingers into Bashir's strong back, becomes one with him, rises up. To the place that is the beginning and the end. Of Everything and Nothing.

Samira and Bashir hold one another, lie in a close embrace, silently. Until the sun casts its first light and its first warmth over the mountains of the Hindu Kush and Samira sees what she had already felt with her fingers in the dark of night. The war has made her friend a man. A real man.

Bashir sees what he had already recognised in the darkness of the night, his friend Samir is even more handsome than all the memories he had carried within him.

Before, Samira had been the taller of the two, now it is Bashir. Bashir has the broader neck, the more powerful back, the stronger arms. A little beard is growing beneath his chin, his curls are full and black. His eyes are dark and full of the heat of longing, full of sad rage.

My eyes have seen war and death, says Bashir. I only endured it because I always had your face before my eyes.

Samira lays her hand on her friend's eyes, says, your eyes are like my father's eyes, full of the pain, known only to men who have killed other men and looked death in the eye themselves. Come with me.

Samira jumps from the rock. It is as it was before, she goes ahead and he follows. She leads, he does not ask. Samira climbs up and down until they come to a small, hidden meadow. Fresh, clear water flows from a rock, collects in a dip and flows on.

Wash yourself, says Samira. The water will heal you, it will drive the pictures from your head and take them away.

Bashir obeys, takes off his clothes, climbs into the water. Samira sits down, pulls off her boots, dangles her feet in the water.

Come to me, says Bashir.

Samira obeys, takes off her waistcoat, not her *kamiz* and her *shalvar*, and steps into the water.

After all that has happened, are you still ashamed? asks Bashir. Come on. Take your clothes off. Bashir throws himself at his friend, tugs at his clothes. Samira defends herself, laughs, Bashir pulls at the fabric tied around her until he has undone it, until he sees Samira's breasts. Bashir utters a stifled cry, throws his hand to his mouth, walks backwards, falls. Samira stops laughing, sees the shock, the fear in her friend's eyes. She grabs her clothes, disappears with them behind the rocks, puts them on, comes back, keeps silent.

You are a woman, says Bashir.

Bale, says Samira.

I didn't know that, says Bashir.

But up there on the rock, up there when you . . . Samira speaks no further.

Bashir does not want her to go on, says, I know. But I didn't know . . . Bashir speaks no further.

Samira does not want him to say it. She wants to say it herself. You thought you loved a man.

Bale.

And now that you know I am a woman, do you not love me any more?

Bashir keeps silent. It is as though he is seeing Samira for the first time.

Everything is as it was a moment before. Nothing is as it was a moment before. Bashir knows nothing any more. Understands nothing any more. His world falls, breaks into a thousand and one pieces.

Now you know my secret, says Samira, then falls silent.

The sun takes its light and disappears behind the peak. The stars and the moon have been hanging in the sky for a long time when Bashir says, be without worry. I will sort everything out. I will tell my father, I will tell Gol-Sar. I will get women's clothes for you, from now on you can let your hair grow long and weave it into plaits. From now on it is my turn to protect you.

You will not do that, says Samira. We won't tell anyone anything.

Why not? asks Bashir. I will take you as my wife, we will live together as man and woman and everyone will be happy and contented.

You have lost your reason, says Samira. No one else will be happy and contented, and neither will we.

I will be happy and contented if you will be my wife, says Bashir.

Bashir, my dear friend, says Samira.

Bashir interrupts her. Don't call me that. I am not your friend. I am going to be your husband and you will be my wife.

I will not be your wife. I cannot be, says Samira.

Why not? For what reason can you not be my wife?

Because I am a man, says Samira. Because you and I are friends.

You are not a man. I have seen it, with my own eyes. I have seen your . . . Bashir does not want to say the word, but he says it anyway. I have seen your breasts.

Samira reflects and thinks, thinks and reflects, gets to her feet, walks back and forth, squats on a stone, squats in the meadow, throws stones into the water, draws her dagger, scratches around on the ground with it, finds a piece of wood, carves the wood into a point, makes an arrow of it.

Stop that, says Bashir.

What do you want me to stop? asks Samira, throws the arrow so that it sticks in the ground.

Everything. The throwing, the carving. The squatting on stones like a man. The walking up and down, like a man. The being Samir. You should behave like a woman. You should behave like Samira.

Samira laughs, squats on the stone, her legs wide apart. Like a man. You see? That's what I mean. I am not a woman. I am a man. And I am not your wife. I am your friend. We have been hunting together, we have climbed up the mountain together and fished together, we have fought and gone to school together. We have been two boys. Two real boys. What sort of life will it be if I become your wife?

A life between a man and a woman. A real life, says Bashir, pulls the arrow out of the ground and throws it into the water. The arrow becomes a boat, dances on the water, is carried away by it.

Fine, says Samira. Tell your father. Tell him. First he will shoot me, then my mother, then your sister and finally you. Tell him.

He won't shoot anyone.

For what reason would he not shoot me? I have dared to penetrate the world of men, I have passed myself off as one of them. I go to the bazaar as they do, I strike deals and haggle. I spit as they do, says Samira and spits on the ground like a man. Like a real man. As she always does.

Bashir turns away. Repelled, revolted. He looks at Samira from head to toe, rises up, disappears into the darkness.

Samira stays in the little meadow, walks back and forth, sits by the water, plays her feet in it, rewraps the fabric around her chest, gets dressed, rides back to her tent.

Daria sits by her fire, pulls bread out of the oven. She says, you are just in time, the bread is ready. Come, my child, sit down, have some tea, it will do you good.

Samira squats down, does not know how to begin to tell her what has happened. She does not want to worry her mother, but knows she must tell her, because if Bashir actually does what he says he is going to do, it will not be long before Commander Rashid comes and shoots her and her mother.

Samira tells her mother everything, becomes the child from Before, plays with the brightly coloured fabric of her mother's dress. Daria finds her reason. Not for long, only for a short time. She sees the confusion in the eyes of her daughter-son, does something she has not done for a long time. She takes Samira in her arms, kisses her on the forehead. Samira does something she has not done for a long time, lays her head in her mother's lap, weeps.

Then let them kill us, says Daria and laughs. What difference does it make whether we live or are dead?

Daria lies under her blankets and does not go to sleep. Samira is squatting outside her tent playing her flute, when Bashir comes riding up.

Have you told them? asks Samira. Have you come to kill me?

Bashir looks at her, says, you are stealing my reason. You can do with me what you want. I am not going to tell anyone anything. But you tell me what I should do. Tell me how my life should be. You always have done. So tell me now. He looks at Samira, digs around in the earth with his knife, waits for an answer.

I've never told you to go to war. You went anyway.

My father wanted it this way. We had no money. What do I know? I don't know anything any more. Samir. Samira. I don't even know what to call you. I don't know any more who it is I love. Who is it that I have carried around in my heart for all these years? Who is it that I talk to now?

You did not go to war because you wanted to earn money, says Samira. You went to war because you wanted to be a man and come back to me as a real man.

Bashir keeps silent.

Let's leave everything as it is, says Samira. We will see what happens.

Samira and Bashir do as Samira says, they leave everything as it is and see what happens.

Samira remains Samir. Samir and Gol-Sar remain engaged. Samir and Bashir remain friends. Bashir continues to call Samira Samir. Samira keeps going to hunt, sells fish, meat and hides. Bashir does not want to go hunting, but he goes along anyway when Samira goes into the village, to the stream or anywhere else. Bashir goes with her no matter where she goes.

Now that her brother has come back, and spends all his time with her fiancé, Gol-Sar no longer dares to go and see Samira in secret on her rock at night. But she is not stupid, and her longing for her Samir is so great that she finds ways to see Samira in secret.

So Samira lives two secrets, one with Gol-Sar and one with Bashir.

The days become birds, flock together and fly away.

Bashir, say the men, people say the foreigners have women who are soldiers. Did you meet any of them? Were they pretty? Did you look them in the eye? Why did you not invite them up here? You should have married one of them, it would have been better for you than marrying one of our girls. The men do not speak to Samira about girls, because after all she is engaged to Gol-Sar, Bashir's sister and their commander's daughter. They would never sully the honour of Gol-Sar and thus of her brother, her father and her fiancé. Only sometimes one of the men says, your bride could lose her patience, when are you finally going to marry her?

Although they are not boys any more, Samira and Bashir still go riding down into the valley every morning as they did before, go to class. They talk, ask questions, give answers, reject old thoughts, learn new ones.

Why do you not teach the children up in the mountains? asks the kindly teacher. He does not say the boys, he says the children. Samira gathers the girls and boys around her, does as the kindly teacher did to her years before. First she teaches the children to write their names. Then every child learns its favourite word. Then they learn a new word made up of the letters in their name and the letters of their favourite word. Samira has got used to squatting under the tree by the stream, playing her flute and waiting until the children come. When the boys and girls can read and write ten and more words, Samira buys exercise books and pencils in the village and gives them to the children.

Some fathers and brothers of the girls are sceptical, want to see with their own eyes what is going on at the stream between Samir and their little daughters. The brothers and fathers come to the stream, squat down, listen, see that nothing bad is happening, are contented. Some fathers and brothers stay in the class themselves, learn how to write their names and their favourite words.

Come with me, says Samira to her mother. I want you to come to my class. I want you to find your reason again. I want you to take care of Gol-Sar in case I am not there for her one day.

Daria obeys. Goes along. Always. Whenever Samira says, I'm going to the stream to see the children, Daria pulls her scarf over her head, goes with her, sits down and learns everything that her daughter-son has to teach the children.

By now so many boys are coming to school down in the village that the kindly teacher cannot teach them all. He laughs, pushes his tied-together spectacles up his nose, says, after all these years people have finally worked out that fighting and killing get us nowhere. That is good, says the kindly teacher and smiles. May God will that they do not think you can learn to know things as quickly as you can learn to kill.

The kindly teacher knows that many fathers would give their daughters permission to come to school if a woman were teaching them. Samira tells him about Gol-Sar, who has secretly learned to read and write, she is even reading proper books.

Bring her along, says the kindly teacher.

Her father will shoot me, says Samira.

Then bring her along when you have married her, when she is your wife and you are in charge, says the kindly teacher.

I will, says Samira. She lowers her eyes to avoid to have to look her teacher in the eye.

Everything is fine the way it is. Everyone is content. Everyone is happy. Until the day that the kindly teacher says, Samir, my boy, you are no longer a child. You are a strong and bright man. It is time for you to make a decision. It is time to live out your dream. It is time for you to think of your future.

The future will come soon enough, says Samira.

The future came a long time ago, says the kindly teacher. Here in the mountains, here in this little village, here in the middle of nowhere you have no future. Go. Listen to me. Go.

Where am I to go?

Go where you can learn a profession, where you can make your dreams come true.

Where is that place?

If I knew where that place was, I would not be here.

How am I to find that place, if you have not found it? asks Samira.

You are different from me, says the kindly teacher.

Samira smiles.

You are stronger than me, you are . . . the kindly teacher does not speak further, searches in his head for words that he cannot find, finds them, says, you are the kind of person that the world needs. You are . . . again the kindly teacher searches for words, finds them, says, you bear within you the courage of a man and the kindness of a woman.

Samira does not smile any more. She lowers her eyes, draws lines in the sand with her finger, rubs them out again. Samira reflects, knows it would be foolish to tell the kindly teacher the truth about Samira and Samir. But Samira also knows that the only person in the whole of the Hindu Kush that she could trust, the only person who could help her, is the kindly teacher. She looks at him and says, I am not the Samir you think you know.

The kindly teacher smiles and says, that too is a virtue that I esteem in you. You are modest.

I am not modest, says Samira. I have just learned to play the game.

The kindly teacher smiles, looks at his pupil, does not smile any more, asks, what game are you talking about?

The game of life.

If you could only hear yourself, you do not know the impact of your own words. It would be a waste for you to stay here.

Samira lowers her eyes and swallows down tears, says, do not talk about me like that. My shoulders are heavy with guilt.

Let's talk about everything another time. Think about what I have said to you.

Samira thinks. Samira thinks much and often about the words of the kindly teacher. Even if she does not intend to do so, she does. With his words, the kindly teacher has found a heavy door somewhere deep inside Samira and pushed it open. However much she might try, however much she pushes and pushes against the door, she cannot close it again. And she had not even known that such a door existed. Since she learned that, nothing else has any importance. Riding is no longer flying, the upland is no longer the loveliest place that Samira can imagine, the happiness that Bashir and Gol-Sar put in her heart is no longer the only happiness that Samira wishes for herself.

You are ungrateful, says the invisible listener. Everything is fine the way it is. You have enough to eat. You have work. People like you. You are alive.

Samira squats on her rock. Alone. Without Bashir. Without Gol-Sar. She wants to be alone. Does not want to speak. To no one. Wants to think.

She goes to the kindly teacher. Squats with him under the tree, listens to him, talks to him.

I have no dream that I could live.

You have many dreams, says the kindly teacher. I know that. I can see them. You have them deep within you. You just do not know it yet.

A PLAN

What are you going to do when you are married?

All I want is to make you happy and content, says Gol-Sar and smiles. A smile that forces Samira to smile as well. Samira pushes the smile aside, tries not to lose the clarity in her head. Tell me what you will do if I am not there one day.

Gol-Sar opens her eyes wide, asks her fiancé where he is thinking of going to, asks him if he wants to leave her. Asks if he has found another wife. Samira hugs little Gol-Sar in her arms, assures her that she is not going anywhere, says that God's ways are unknowable and no one can ever really know what will happen.

Gol-Sar has tears in her eyes, says, I will do whatever you want me to.

Samira grabs her by the arms, shakes her, half full of impotence and half full of rage. Fine, then I will tell you what I want from you. I want you to teach the girls and women to read and write. That's what I want you to do.

And what am I to do for you? asks Gol-Sar. I want to make you happy.

Samira strikes the rock with the flat of her hand, looks into the distance, looks at Gol-Sar again, says, that's what you are to do for me. Just that. You are to teach the girls and the women. That's how you'll make me happy.

Gol-Sar loses her smile, lowers her eyes, nods. If that is your desire, I will do it.

And I want you to go down into the village and teach the girls and women there, too.

Then Samira speaks to Commander Rashid. At first he laughs. He thinks it is unnecessary for women to be able to read and write. The commander does not see the point of it. He thinks girls must follow their men and bring up their children. Only when Samira says there have been enough wars and dead, only when she starts talking about the future of the homeland, only then does the commander not laugh any more. Only when Samira says boys can only be real men if their mothers are bright, only then does the commander stop laughing. Only when Samira says that Daria will accompany Gol-Sar so that people do not speak ill of her, only then does the commander nod. Only when Samira says it is good for his grandchildren to be able to read and write, only then does the commander say he will think about it. Only when Samira says she wants Gol-Sar to start teaching now, that she does not want to wait for the commander to think about it, only then does Commander Rashid say, then you will marry her this summer.

Samira was expecting that. I will, she says, shakes hands with the commander, says, on the life of your sons and your grandsons, swear that you will never forbid her to teach girls and women. Swear on Bashir's life that you will stand by your promise, even if I am no longer with her.

The commander strokes his beard smooth, asks, how

long does it take for someone to be able to read and write?

A long time. It takes a whole lifetime.

So it will be a lifetime before my daughter can read and write herself. By then heaven and earth may well have swapped places. By then I may no longer be alive myself.

Sometimes it happens very quickly, too, says Samira. Some people learn to read and write quickly.

We shall see what happens, says the commander.

You swore on the life of Bashir and your other sons and grandsons. Samira's eyes pierce the commander's eyes, his head, his heart.

The commander presses his lips together, says nothing, just nods.

The same day Samira drags Gol-Sar and her mother along with her from one *kuchi* family to the next, sends them into the tents of the women and girls. Daria and Gol-Sar tell the women they must come to the stream, that they can learn to read and write there. Some women agree. Others ask what they will get in return. Some women say their husbands will not allow it, others say their hands are full already bringing up children and baking bread, making carpets and all sorts of other things. The next day Daria and Gol-Sar are squatting by the stream. At first two women come, then another two, then a few girls and finally even the former girl prostitute comes with all her children. Whether the *Hadji* minds her coming she does not know. Either he permits it or he doesn't, she says. And if he doesn't allow it, and scolds, then let him scold. Now I'm here, let's see what happens.

Life has made you a fighter, you are brave, says Samira.

Samira speaks to the kindly teacher, speaks to the men in the village, goes from one to the other, talks to the butcher and the mullah, the *rish-sefid* and even the disgusting vegetable-seller. She collects money from each of them. The men cannot or do not want to pay a great deal, but it places them under an obligation and binds them to their word. With the money and the help of a few young and old men from the village, Samira builds four mud walls next to the room where the boys are being taught. When they reach to her knees, Samira gathers all the important and all the unimportant men from the village and also asks Commander Rashid to come. Samira says the men have come to thank the honoured commander.

The commander is amazed. Why do the men want to thank me?

They want to thank you for giving your daughter permission to come to the village and give an education to their daughters in this room here. Samira says that, and then everything is quiet. So quiet that all the men can hear the commander's breath.

At that very moment, when neither the other men nor the commander know what to say or do, someone calls, long live the commander and his far-sightedness and his love for his people and his homeland.

It is the boy with no legs who says it. The boy who is no longer a boy but a young man. After his shouting long live the commander, the young man applauds. The other men do as he does, applaud too. At first the commander is suspicious, at first Samira does not know if he is going to get angry. But then all the boys and men come to him, want to shake his hand, slap him on the shoulder, admire him.

The commander looks round at everyone, says, before this mud becomes real walls, and the girls can be taught by my daughter, there is a great deal of work to be done. You need to hurry. He reaches into his scarf, pulls out a few banknotes and gives them to Samira.

Many days and nights come and go before the commander actually keeps his word and allows his daughter to go down into the village. Still more days and nights come and go before Gol-Sar and Daria actually dare to go into the village. Many more days and nights come and go before the fathers and eldest brothers, uncles and mullahs allow a few girls to go to Gol-Sar and Daria's lessons.

But the day comes. The day when a few girls come to class, shyly and with their heads hidden under scarves. The girls are accompanied by their brothers and fathers, they cling to the men or one of the other girls. They come into the little room, sit on the floor. At first they do not take off their scarves, at first they do not talk, at first they just sit there with their eyes lowered. At first they do not understand anything that Gol-Sar says to them, all they understand is their own insecurity, their own fear. They do not understand why all of a sudden it is right which was forbidden until yesterday. For what reason they have been given permission all of a sudden to go out into the street, when until only yesterday they had to stay behind the doors of their huts?

At first only Gol-Sar and Daria speak. They speak quietly, because they are not used to talking to strangers. Because they are not used to speaking unasked. Then they speak. The girls raise their arms, talk quietly at first, then loudly, they laugh, sing and finally they ask questions. At first the girls keep to themselves, then they play and talk with the boys as well.

It's time for you to keep your side of the promise, says Commander Rashid.

Samira agrees, says she will marry Gol-Sar when the moon once more has grown thin and then round again.

Bashir is confused. He does not know what it all means, all this classroom-building, all this sending Gol-Sar into the village, all this 'I'm-going-to-marry-her' business. Bashir does not know what the one has to do with the other, how Samira wants to solve the problems that with the marriage she is inevitably going to run into. Because marriage involves the marital duty of turning one's bride into a woman and to satisfy her, and to plant sons in her belly.

Trust me, says Samira. Be patient. When the time has come I will tell you everything.

Bashir looks up at the moon. You have not all that much time left.

I know, says Samira.

The days become birds, flock together and fly away. The commander, Gol-Sar's mother, Gol-Sar herself, are all preoccupied with the preparations for the marriage. The bride collects pearls and sequins and sews them on to her new dress. Sews on mirrors that are supposed to protect her against the evil eye, and misfortune. Her mother stirs henna to keep the bride's blood from overheating. The men slaughter a goat, the boys spread carpets on the meadow, the women decorate the bride's tent.

I have always found a way, says Samira. I will find one now, too.

You want to marry my sister. That is not a good way, says Bashir. She will find out that you are not a man.

She will not, says Samira. At first I thought the best thing would be for me to go away. But that would have broken Gol-Sar's heart, the people would have talked behind her back, and your father would have avenged himself on my mother. Marriage is the only way.

And how are you going to keep Gol-Sar from noticing that you are not a man?

I will be her husband only for one night.

And then? asks Bashir. What will you do after that one night?

I will die, says Samira.

You have lost your reason, says Bashir. I will not allow it. And what sort of consolation is that supposed to be for poor Gol-Sar? Her husband killing himself? People will say, Gol-Sar couldn't make her husband happy, that is why he took his own life. They will say it is Gol-Sar's fault.

I will not kill myself, says Samir. I will go into the mountains, step on a mine and die. I will become a *shahid* of war. And the honour of my martyr's death will transfer to my wife.

Bashir does not know whether to laugh or cry, whether to hit his friend or run away, whether he should be silent or do something else. Bashir hugs Samira. Not like a friend, not like a boy. He hugs her as a real man hugs a real woman. He undresses her and makes love to her as a real man makes love to a real woman. It is different from before, they both know what they are doing. It does not just happen, they want it. Samira and Bashir make love to each other as they will never again.

Bashir is the first to break the long silence. He strokes Samira's hair, says, if she does not bleed it will mean she's a virgin, then it will be as though she had not married.

I know, says Samira. Trust me.

Bashir speaks in a voice that Samira does not know. I have always loved you. And I love you now, too. Even if I don't know who it is that I love, Samir or Samira. But one thing I swear to you, as surely as I am a man, Gol-Sar is my sister. If you hurt so much as a hair on her head, if you insult her honour or that of my father, then you insult my honour as well. I will kill you. I will have to do it. You know that.

A cold snake enters Samira's belly and devours all the warmth, devours everything that was in Samira. Devours Samira, who, in Samir, had begun to have a face.

A SOLUTION

Gol-Sar's mother has smeared so much henna on her daughter's hands and feet, her neck and her back, that the other women laugh and say, the poor girl's blood will be so cold that she will not notice anything at all on the first night with her handsome husband.

In the night, when Samira and Gol-Sar are alone, Samira hugs her wife, kisses her, looks into her eyes and says, listen to me.

Gol-Sar glows and listens to her husband. Her Samir. The most handsome, the strongest and bravest man the Hindu Kush has ever seen.

Whatever may happen, says Samira, you should know I love, honour and revere you. I took you as my wife because I wanted it. I wanted it because you are unlike all the other girls. I took you as my wife because you have dreams, because you want to make more of your life than just being the wife of a man and pull his sons out of your body.

Gol-Sar opens her mouth, wants to say something. Samira puts her hand to her lips, gently, full of tenderness.

Gol-Sar listens.

I want you to go on teaching the girls, says Samira. I want you to become a good teacher. I want you to go into the village, to be more than only a woman. You shall be a human being.

Gol-Sar keeps silent, does not know why she does not like how Samir speaks to her.

And never forget, says Samira, wherever I may be, whatever I do or do not do, whether I am alive or dead, you will be a part of me. For ever and eternally and beyond eternity.

Do not speak that way, says Gol-Sar. You are frightening me.

Be without fear. Do not be afraid of anything or anyone. Not even death. Neither mine nor yours. Do not be afraid of life. Be afraid of only one thing. Of not living your life.

Gol-Sar does not understand, plays with the fabric of her dress, wants to lean on the strong shoulder of the man she longs for.

Samira takes off her amulet, ties it round Gol-Sar's neck, says, I have a present for you. It has helped me and protected me. Now it shall protect you and destroy anything and anyone that seeks to harm you.

Gol-Sar touches the amulet, wants to kiss her Samir. Samira draws back, walks up and down in the tent, thinks and ponders.

Come to me, says Gol-Sar. Do not be afraid. I know more than the other girls. I know what happens on a wedding night.

Samira takes off her waistcoat, takes off her glittering cap, pulls off her father's boots.

Come to me, says Gol-Sar. Come and make me your wife, so that our marriage is consummated.

Samira looks at Gol-Sar, can hardly breathe, turns down the oil lamp, lies down beside her. Slowly, very slowly, they touch each other, stroke and kiss each other.

Actually I am frightened, says Gol-Sar.

I am frightened too, says Samira.

The women say it will hurt. Gol-Sar gulps and says, let's wait.

Don't be afraid. I won't hurt you. Never. Samira is ashamed, wants to die, prays for forgiveness for her guilt, swallows down tears, cannot hide them, weeps, sighs.

Gol-Sar does not see Samira's tears, leans her head back, groans, arches her body, her eyes closed. Gol-Sar laughs quietly, is full of happiness, says, it does not hurt. It is beautiful. There is a lump in Samira's throat, it presses, pushes and takes the air to breathe away. Gol-Sar laughs. A snake enters Samira's belly. At first it's only a pain-snake, then comes the fear-snake then the grief-snake and finally the fourth snake, the blood-snake.

Gol-Sar bleeds, is no longer a girl, is a woman.

The taste of poison comes into Samira's mouth. The taste of lust for life comes into Gol-Sar's mouth. The taste of being a woman. Gol-Sar is full of happiness-snakes, pleasure-snakes, good snakes. Gol-Sar laughs. Samira weeps. Quietly. Silently, so that Gol-Sar does not notice. So that Samira's four snakes do not startle Gol-Sar's many snakes. So that Gol-Sar does not lose her happiness. So that Gol-Sar does not lose face, so that her honour is assured. So that Samira does not heap yet more guilt upon herself. Gol-Sar sleeps. Samira prays, asks for forgiveness. Gol-Sar dreams. Samira feels her guilt.

Before the sun comes over the mountain with its first light and its first warmth, Samira lays the little white cloth, which is no longer white, which is decorated with Gol-Sar's woman's blood, next to the sleeping figure. So that Gol-Sar has the proof that she had been a virgin, that she has become a woman. Woman's blood that proves Samira's manhood.

Samira kisses Gol-Sar on the forehead, strokes her hair, pulls on her father's boots, creeps to her mother's tent, wakes her, hugs her, kisses her, tells her her plan.

Daria finds her reason, looks at her daughter-son, says, my clever child. I knew you would find a way.

Samira speaks quietly, in a voice without fear. Mother, see Gol-Sar as the daughter you never had. Find your own life. I know you can do it. Find the world and help Gol-Sar to know it. Help Gol-Sar to understand that she does not need a man to be a woman. A real woman. Find your reason. Walk by her side.

Daria runs her hand over her daughter's hair, gives her a bundle, says, it is time for you to become Samira. Live your life. Live it as you lived the life of Samir, but live it as Samira.

You speak well, says Samira. She looks at her mother, swallows down tears, says thank you.

Daria takes her child in her arms, presses her to her heart, does not want to let her go. Never again.

When Samira returns to her marriage tent, Bashir is already waiting for her. Together they creep past the tents of the other *kuchi*, steal the *Hadji*'s biggest billy-goat, carry it into the mountains, tether it firmly, come back.

In the morning the *Hadji* rages noisily when he sees his biggest billy-goat is gone.

The men from the neighbouring tents come running, want to know what has happened. Some of them look for the goat, others go back to their tents. Samira and Bashir swing on to their horses. We will find him, they say and ride off.

Samira does not ride quickly, does not fly, drags herself, the bundle that her mother gave her, and a bundle that she has packed herself. Samira sees the tents, sees the other *kuchi*, the meadow, the stream, the animals, the flowers, she sees the mountains, sees her rock, sees all that and much more, knows this is the last time. Samira and Bashir climb up the mountain, untether the *Hadji's* billy-goat and lead it by the rope. The billy-goat looks odd. Samira has shorn the poor creature, its belly, its back, its sides. The billy-goat is naked. Its skin looks like the bare skin of a human being. Only the head and tail of the billy-goat are still hairy.

A shame about the billy-goat, says Samira.

The old *Hadji* deserved it, says Bashir, tries to laugh, cannot.

Samira takes off her waistcoat with its pearls and mirrors, takes off her *shalvar-kamiz*, takes off her father's boots, kisses them, takes off her glittering cap, puts on the new things from her bundle. She knots and ties her old clothes around the billy-goat's body.

The explosion is neither particularly big nor particularly loud, but it can be heard all the way down to the tents. Commander Rashid, Daria, Gol-Sar, all the other *kuchi* hear it. They all look up to the mountain from where the explosion has come, they see the smoke and the dust rising into the sky.

Commander Rashid, the *Hadji* and a few other men jump on to their horses, dash off. Women and girls run around, scream, cry, weep. Women lower their eyes, put their hands to their hearts, others pick up their little children. Children shout and cry. Girls throw their hands to their mouths, run towards the explosion. Gol-Sar looks at her mother, goes into her marriage tent, fetches the little cloth with the blood, gives it to her mother.

The men arrive at the bottom of the mountain. The commander sees his son, jumps from his horse, gives thanks to God that he is alive. Bashir is carrying an enormous lump, a confusion of clothes, the remains of boots, flesh, skin, mirrors and pearls that are supposed to protect against the evil eye and all kinds of misfortune. Blood, dirt, earth, the shattered head of the billy-goat. Everything is stuck together. Blood drips. Rags fall to the ground. The commander runs over to his son, sees the grief, the fear, the pain, takes his *patu* off his shoulders, lays it on the ground, takes the confusion of flesh and blood, dirt and rags from his son, lays them in the *patu*. Other men roll up the *patu*, lift it on to the back of a horse. The *Hadji* is sorry that his goat also died when Samir caught it in order to bring it back to him, but then, together with the animal, stepped on the mine.

The commander stands in front of his son, does not take his eyes off him, grips him by the arms, pulls him to him, presses him to his heart, weeps. Bashir trembles, cries, hugs his father, holds him tight. Very tight. Never wants to let go of him. Never again.

The commander knows he has never before held his son. The son knows his father will never do it again. Bashir falls silent. It's a silence that is the beginning of everything. The beginning and the end. The beginning of father and son. The end.

Daria weeps, cries, tears her hair, throws herself on the ground, scratches her face till it bleeds. Real blood. Daria weeps. Weeps for her lost commander, weeps for the son that she never pulled out of her body, for the lost girl she never had. Daria weeps for her lost father, for the lost mother she has never wept for. Daria weeps for the answers she never gave to Samira. Daria weeps for Samira and Samir, for her lost reason, for her lost life.

Gol-Sar has lost the colour from her face, her lips tremble, she squats by the *patu* that the men have laid outside her tent, stares at it, wants to open it. The commander seizes his daughter, holds her. Gol-Sar lets him, does not resist, goes on staring at the *patu*, does not move, does not weep. Does not weep for her lost husband who was her husband for only one night.

Bashir squats next to Gol-Sar, stares at his sister, takes her in his arms, whispers quietly in her ear, he is alive. Gol-Sar looks at her brother, smiles. It is a tiny smile that she quickly loses again. A smile that melts into a weep. Gol-Sar says, I know. He lives on here. Here in my heart. And I live in his heart. He told me. He foresaw his death.

Before the sun disappears behind the mountain with its last light and its last warmth, the men dig a hole, lay the *patu* with the scraps of dead Samir in the hole, cover it, pile a mound of earth over it. Gol-Sar and Bashir, the commander and Daria and the other *kuchi* squat around the mound of earth, pray, weep. When the other *kuchi* go, when the stars come, when only Daria, the commander, Bashir, Gol-Sar and Gol-Sar's mother are still sitting by the mound of earth, Gol-Sar asks for the little white cloth with her blood. Her mother does not want to give it to her, is ashamed, her brother and father are not supposed to see it, after all, they are men. Her father says, give it to her. Her mother obeys. Gol-Sar fills the white cloth with earth from the mound of earth under which her husband lies, empties it again, fills it up with earth again, empties it. Four times. Then she fills it with earth again, puts it on her head. Gol-Sar's mother says, she has lost her reason, wants to take the cloth away from her daughter. Bashir grips his mother's hand, says, leave her alone. Her mother leaves her alone, stands up, goes. Commander Rashid and Bashir go. Daria and Gol-Sar stay. It is as it was before. This time it is not Samira, this time it is Gol-Sar who lays her head in Daria's lap.

A DEFEAT

The days and nights come and go, turn into birds, flock together and fly away. Daria and Gol-Sar go down to the village every day, give lessons to the girls, teach them to read and write. Gol-Sar looks at Daria, smiles. Daria looks at Gol-Sar, smiles. Your son told me to live, says Gol-Sar, and tries to live. He said I should be afraid only of not living my life. Gol-Sar looks into the distance as though her Samir were standing there. I am living, she says. As well as I can.

Daria runs her hand over Gol-Sar's hair, says, you are.

The days come and go, become birds, flock together and fly away. Bashir has told his father he is going to look for work, in Pakistan, or Iran, or wherever else. He is long gone. Neither to Pakistan, nor to Iran, nor elsewhere. Bashir rides into the mountains, rides back to Samira.

Samira has undone her mother's bundle, it has a dress in it, brightly coloured as a field on which flowers grow, with a thousand and one pearls and mirrors. It has a yellow scarf in it to cover her hair, her shoulders and her breasts. Samira sits by the clothes for a long time, looks at them, touches them, plays with them. She holds the scarf in the wind, makes it flutter and dance as though it were a flag. She holds the dress in front of her body, looks down at herself. At the end of all the scarf-waving and dress-holding, she bundles up her Samir clothes, puts the women's clothes on, combs her man's hair out of her face, ties it back, drapes the scarf over her head, sits down, puts her gun in her lap and waits. When Bashir comes back to her, Samira does not move, she does not speak, just looks at Bashir. Bashir says, they believed it and they think you are dead. They wept. They will get over it.

Khoda-ra shokr, thanks be to God, says Samira.

What are we going to do? asks Bashir.

We're going to ride and see where the paths takes us, says Samira.

In the first village where no one knows them, Bashir wants to go to the mullah and take Samira as his wife. But Samira still does not know how to become the wife of a man whose friend she has just been. She does not know how to live without fishing and hunting, without going to school or the bazaar, without all that and much else besides. Bashir does not want Samira to take off her women's clothes again. He wants her to try. He wants them to see what happens.

Samira and Bashir try that.

In the next village Bashir the man and Samira the woman ride down the main street, slowly, without swirling up the sand in the street, they ride past the men in their shops, the tea-houses where men sit and drink tea. Samira and Bashir do not know why the men are looking at them in alarm and horror, until a boy points at Samira and says, look, that's her. That's the woman with the gun over her shoulder. Samira takes her gun off her shoulder. They ride on.

In the next village they find a dal-seller. They know the proper thing to do. Bashir buys two bowls of dal, takes them over to Samira, who sits on the ground in a side-alley like a decent woman, hidden from the gaze of strange men, with her face covered, as she waits for her Bashir. Samira and Bashir eat, drink tea. Everything is fine. Samira is a woman, Bashir a man.

In the next village Bashir wants to go to the mullah and take Samira as his wife. Samira gives in, they go to the mullah, he speaks his *be-isme-Allah* and other prayers and makes them into man and wife before God.

On the way to the next village they see a mountain goat. It is as it always is when the two of them see a goat. They whistle through their teeth, shove their heels into the flanks of their horses, urge them on, ride at the animal from both sides, shoot. Bashir is the first to hit the goat with his bullet. The injured animal flees in the other direction to escape from the line of fire, towards Samira. She jumps from the stallion, throws herself at the goat, pulls it to the ground, draws her dagger, slits its throat with a quick cut, frees it from its death-struggle. It is as it has always been. Samira gives the sacrificial blood to the earth beneath her feet, so that God's blessing will accompany her on her journey. Together Samira and Bashir strip the animal of its skin, cut up the hide, take the body apart, cut up the meat as they learned from the butcher, roll up the hide, bring the meat and the hide to the nearest village to sell it while it is still fresh.

The butcher scratches his beard and looks first at Bashir, then at Samira, who is standing modestly behind him, asks, is that your wife? Bashir does not turn round, does not look at Samira, looks at the butcher, does not smile, says *bale*.

The butcher says, she has blood on her dress. People say it was her who slit the goat's throat.

Bashir does not know what to say, just looks at the butcher.

The butcher says, people say she rode like a man, she jumped from the horse and threw herself on the goat, pulled it to the ground and slit its throat.

Bashir opens his mouth, closes it again, does not know what to say. Samira pushes her way in front of Bashir, props her hands on her hips, says, I have a gun, I shoot, and I slit goats' throats and if it has to be I'll slit yours too and I'll slit the throat of any men who think they know so much and need to talk so much.

The butcher does not want to argue, certainly not with a woman who has a gun and a dagger, and looks as if she knows what to do with them. He would rather pull out of the deal with the meat.

Wars, the drought, the foreigners have all done everything imaginable to our country, says the butcher. And the years that have come and gone have also brought some strange things with them. But anything like this woman? No. God is my witness. Neither I nor any of the other men in the village have ever seen anything like it. And if we are honest, and we are honest, we do not want to see such a thing. Not in our village.

Samira is so full of fury, she wants to leap at the impudent butcher's throat. Bashir is ashamed. He grips Samira by the arm, holds her back, drags her away from the butcher, his shop and the village.

That could have been a good deal, says Bashir.

It is not my fault, says Samira. The bastard insulted me.

He did not, says Bashir. He just said what people had

seen and what they were talking about, because they find it strange for a woman to behave like a man.

The next village is too far away, and as the meat will not stay fresh in the heat, Samira and Bashir give it to the people they meet along the way. They ride on. Everything is fine until they cross the next upland plain. Even from a distance, Samira recognises the shouts of the men, their whistles, the stamping and thundering of the hooves of a hundred and more horses and their riders. It is the music of a game. The game of games. She holds the reins of her stallion tight. The horse wants to go to the game, wants to go charging off, shakes its head up and down, so that its mane dances. Samira does not know why everything happens as it does. She does not intend to whistle through her teeth, to shove her heels into her stallion's sides, Samira does not intend to urge the stallion on. But she does. She charges off, crosses the river. The water splashes high, and she dashes across the plain. The stallion snorts, its hooves thunder against the ground as though it wanted to ram them into the earth. God sends his *houris*, they carry the stallion on their wings. Wind flies under Samira's yellow scarf, it billows up, Samira gallops, charges, flies, makes short little cries, whistles through her teeth, dashes past the players, dashes towards the knot of men, the stallion rears up on its hind legs, some of the other horses start back, the stallion plunges into their midst, lowers its head, raises it, opens its eyes and its mouth, looks like a monster. The men cannot believe their eyes. At first they assume the woman in their midst has lost control of her horse, has lost her mind. Samira guides her stallion to the spot where the other riders throng around the dead calf, pulls her foot from the stirrup, holds tight on to the horse's mane, reaches for the calf, clutches its hide, lifts the carcass, it slips, falls to the ground. One of the men roars, takes his short whip between his teeth, bends down, grabs the calf, cannot get hold of it because Samira's stallion again has taken up position over the dead animal. Samira knows the men have worked out by now that she has neither lost control of her horse, nor lost her mind. She lowers herself along the side of her horse once again, the stallion holds its large head protectively over her slender woman's body, she claws her hand into the dead hide, pulls it to her, the horse takes four steps forward, lifts its head, whinnies, takes another four steps, rides off. The horse has emerged from the knot of horses and human beings long before the other riders notice that the calf is no longer in the *helal* circle. Only now does Samira straighten up, wedge the calf between her thighs and the stallion's powerful back. The folds of her wide skirt get muddled, spill over the calf. While Samira is dashing over the plain she loses her yellow scarf, it goes flying through the air. Samira presses herself down firmly into her saddle, wraps her reins around the calf's leg, dashes as quickly as she can to the flag. Samira turns round, a hundred and more men are chasing her, are closer behind her than she had thought. She loosens the reins even further, bends down even lower, and lets her stallion do the rest. Only one rider catches up with her, rides alongside her. With eyes full of fury, he looks into Samira's eyes, the eyes of a woman. The flag is only four horse-lengths away from her. The stallion stamps its hooves into the ground, stretches its neck, dashes as though its life depended on it. Samira rides round the flag and back to the circle that is *helal*. It is as though the rest of the players are no longer in the field,

Samira dashes past them, knocks them over, does not get out of their way, rides straight at them. The other men's horses make way, rear up on their back legs, throw their riders. Samira comes to the circle that is *helal*, does not throw the calf but sets it down, her eyes find the referee, she bows first to the calf, then to the referee, shoves her heels into her stallion's sides, urges it on, dashes from the playing-field and across the plain. She races to the mountains, urges her stallion on between the rocks until she is sure no one is coming after her. The stallion snorts, raises and lowers its head, its hide is damp and warm, Samira laughs. Laughs until she cries. Samira has won. She has been in the real game, beaten a hundred and more men, she knows there is nothing, nothing, that she cannot achieve. Samira knows she has pushed open the door within her.

Did you see? asks Samira when Bashir finds her. Samira jumps up, laughs, kisses Bashir, hops up and down as little Samira did, throws herself into Bashir's arms as she threw herself into the arms of her commander father.

Bashir grabs Samira by the collar, pulls and tugs at her, yells at her, hits her in the face, throws her on the ground, throws himself on top of her, squats on her chest, presses down on her throat, looks at her with eyes full of rage. Full of rage and hatred. You have lost your mind. You are like your mother. Without reason.

Samira does not defend herself, lies where she is, just looks at Bashir until he lets go of her, stands up, turns away from her. Samira beats the dust from her dress, sees the tear in the fabric, stands in front of Bashir, opens her mouth, wants to say something, does not know which of the many words she wants to say. She should say. Says nothing, then she does as Bashir has done, grabs him by the collar, looks at him, does not hit him, kisses him. Samira kisses Bashir full on the mouth. It is a kiss unlike any kiss she has ever given anyone before. Samira did not know there could be a kiss like that. Strictly speaking, Samira does not even know whether what she is doing with her mouth is a kiss at all. Many years will come and go before Samira knows that what happened between her and Bashir that day was actually a kiss. A real kiss. Between a real woman and a real man.

Who was it, who did that? asks Bashir. Samir or Samira?

Samira shrugs, smiles, says *man che midanam*, swings on to the back of her stallion, whistles through her teeth, rides down the mountain, urges the stallion on, drives him down the path into the gully.

In the days that come and go Samira makes a real effort. She does not want to act like a man. She wants to stop being a man, she wants to be a woman. A real woman. Samira is silent in public, does not wear her gun over her shoulder, does not jump from the horse, does not swing on to the back of her stallion, waits for Bashir to help her to climb on to her horse and get back down again. Whatever she does or does not do, she is constantly looking at Bashir, trying to see in his eyes whether she is behaving like a man or, finally, like a woman.

You walk like a man, you speak like a man, you move like a man, your voice is that of a man, says Bashir.

Is it the woman in me that disgusts you, or the man? asks Samira.

Bashir keeps silent, takes the reins from her hand, leads her stallion. Bashir rides ahead, Samira rides behind him, lowers her head when they meet people or pass through a village. Samira tries to be a real woman. In the evening she collects wood, lights the fire, spreads out the blankets, unpacks the bread and cheese, puts the pot on the fire, sits beside it, puts tea in the pot, fills the glass, hands it to Bashir.

Bashir does not look at Samira when he asks whether she is a real woman inside. Samira does not understand. Bashir does not look at Samira, says, I want to know if you are a real woman in your body, in your belly, I want to know whether you are capable of carrying my son in your belly, pulling him out of your body and giving him milk from your breast.

In the morning, when Bashir wakes up, the fire is not burning any more. The ashes are cold. Samira is still sitting in the same place, still with her back turned to Bashir. Everything is as it was the night before. Nothing is as it was. Samira is no longer wearing her brightly coloured dress, is wearing her men's clothes. Samira does not turn round to Bashir, does not look at him.

We are friends, she says. We have ridden through the mountains together and hunted, we have ridden to the village together and gone to class. Samira laughs. It is a short laugh that she quickly loses. She says, together we saw the disgusting vegetable-seller rubbing his cock, together we brought his opium to the next village, I freed you from the clutches of the man who . . .

Bashir does not want Samira to go on talking. I know, he says.

We have hunted together, says Samira. We have caught fish, we have ridden full tilt across the plain. We will not be able to do any of that if we are not friends any more, if I am your wife and you are my husband.

Bashir knows, he sits down beside Samira, lays his arm around her shoulders, looks into her dark, sad eyes, does not speak much, just says, we have lost our Before.

Their hearts turn to paper. Tear, with a loud rip. Into a thousand pieces. Pieces that they hold in the wind so that they fly. Over all mountains, all valleys, all villages, all people.

Samira does not swallow down her tears. Bashir does not swallow down his tears.

What will you do? asks Bashir.

Samira laughs. Weeps and laughs. It is like Before. When he went to the South and she went to the village. Bashir is forever asking his friend, what are you going to do?

Bashir smiles. He knows what his friend's answer is.

I will do the right thing, says Samira.

Bashir looks into the sky and says, you want to be a *pilot*.

Bashir, my poor Bashir, says Samira. You are a dreamer.

Give me one promise, says Bashir. If you ever become a pilot, fly over our plain and think of us.

First I will fly over the sacred lake, over the upland where my father and I were born, then I will fly over your plain, I will fly away over our rock and call your name.

Are you frightened? asks Bashir.

Yes, says Samira. It is the same Yes as before. A small one. Small, yet full of meaning. Samira says, I stood on the rock, looked my father in the eye and said, I see nothing. It is like Before. I have a dream. I just do not see it.

Samira had a thousand and one questions and not a single answer. Samira stayed mute.

Samira will do the right thing.

She swings on to the back of her father's stallion, urges him on, leaves the Hindu Kush and Bashir behind, does not swallow down her tears, weeps. Weeps until her weeping turns to laughter. It is a laughter that she does not lose quickly, laughter that will stay with her for a long time. It is the laughter of a woman. A real woman.

It is the laughter of Samira.